THE COMPLETE HOLIDAY CELEBRATION

EDITED BY AMY APPLEBY

A treasury of songs arranged for piano/vocal with full lyrics & chords.
Includes many delicious recipes from around the world,
hundreds of delightful illustrations,
and seasonal stories and poems.

AMSCO PUBLICATIONS
NEW YORK • LONDON • SYDNEY

to the memory of Dilson Petrie,
a superb musician and a true friend

Cover photography by Comstock, Inc.
Interior design and layout by Peter Pickow
Paste-up and special graphics by Frank Findley

Copyright © 1994 Amsco Publications,
A Division of Music Sales Corporation, New York, NY.
Portions of this work were previously published in *Celebrate the Bounty*
by Amy Appleby and Jerald B. Stone. Copyright © 1990 by Amy Appleby.

Order No. AM 91477
US International Standard Book Number: 0.8256.1428.7
UK International Standard Book Number: 0.7119.4341.9

Exclusive Distributors:
Music Sales Corporation
257 Park Avenue South, New York, New York 10010 USA
Music Sales Limited
8/9 Frith Street, London W1V 5TZ England
Music Sales Pty. Limited
120 Rothschild Street, Rosebery, Sydney, NSW 2018, Australia

Printed in the United States of America by
Vicks Lithograph and Printing Corporation

Introduction

THE VERY BEST holiday memories are punctuated with music and laughter—and the pleasant company of family and friends. Whether you are planning a party—or organizing a special event for school, community, or church—*The Complete Holiday Celebration* is the single source you need. With over one hundred songs for all seasons, this enormous treasury is sure to be welcome wherever people are singing and playing music together. If you're looking for just the right Christmas carol—or that special song for Thanksgiving, Easter, Hanukkah, St. Patrick's Day, or New Year's Eve, this volume contains the perfect selection.

Of course, good food and delicious treats also make holidays memorable—and *The Complete Holiday Celebration* contains dozens of the delicious recipes that everyone loves best. Here you will find the traditional holiday dishes that have been handed down throughout the years; such as, roast turkey, pumpkin pie, figgy pudding, egg nog, potato latkes, hot cross buns, and Christmas fruitcake, to name just a few. Also included are the songs, poems, and stories that immortalize these traditional foods and their special meanings. In addition, you will also find some tasty new dishes mixed in to spice up your feasting table (and perhaps start some holiday traditions of your own).

Many of the world's great poems were inspired by special holiday memories—and you will be delighted to discover (or rediscover) these classics by Wordsworth, Emerson, Shakepeare, Longfellow, Rossetti, Whitman, Pope, Milton, and others. In addition, you will find story selections by favorite authors such as Charles Dickens, Washington Irving, O. Henry, and Hans Christian Andersen. The magic of these literary gems never wears off—no matter how many times you read them or share them with family and friends.

The Complete Holiday Celebration is not only the perfect song treasury for every holiday throughout the year, it is an invaluable cookbook and literary collection which you will enjoy for years to come. So, gather around and have a joyous New Year, a festive Easter, a delicious Thanksgiving, a happy Hanukkah, and a very merry Christmas.

Table of Contents

The Lowly Manger

The Gifts of the Magi

The Winter's Snow

The Romance of Christmas

HOLIDAYS THROUGHOUT THE YEAR

New Year's Day

Martin Luther King Day

Valentine's Day

Presidents Day

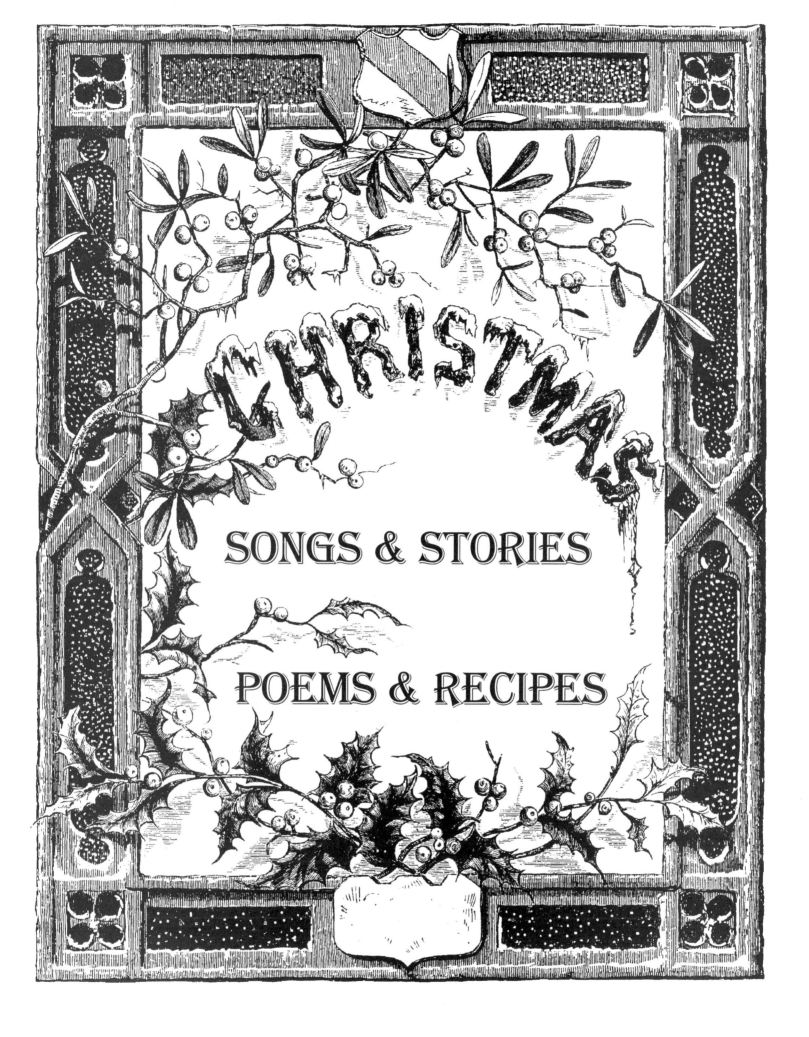

CHRISTMAS

SONGS & STORIES

POEMS & RECIPES

O Come All Ye Faithful

Traditional

Refrain

O come, let us a-dore Him, O come let us a-dore Him, O come let us a-dore Him, Christ the Lord.

2. Sing, choirs of angels, sing in exultation,
O sing all ye citizens of heaven above!
Glory to God, all Glory in the highest.
        Refrain

3. Yea, Lord, we greet Thee, born this happy morning,
Jesus, to Thee be all glory giv'n;
Word of the Father, now in flesh appearing.
        Refrain

God Rest You Merry, Gentlemen

English

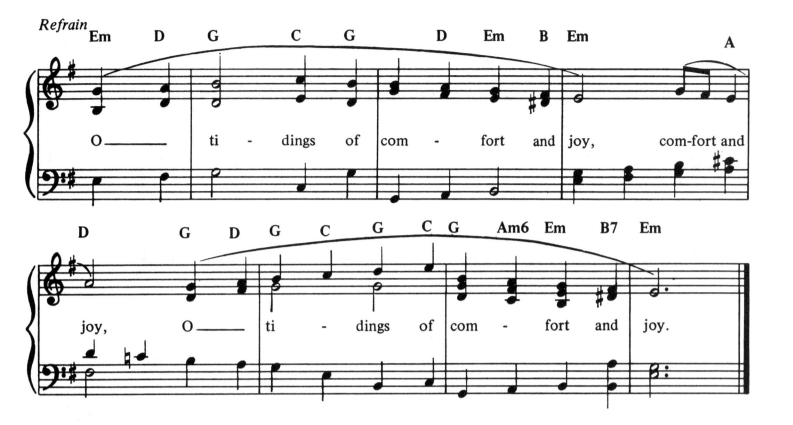

Refrain

O_____ ti - dings of com - fort and joy, com-fort and joy, O_____ ti - dings of com - fort and joy.

2. From God our heavenly Father
   A blessèd angel came.
   And unto certain shepherds
   Brought tidings of the same,
   How that in Bethlehem was born
   The Son of God by name:
   Refrain

3. "Fear not," then said the angel,
   "Let nothing you affright,
   This day is born a Savior,
   Of virtue, power, and might;
   So frequently to vanquish all
   The friends of Satan quite:"
   Refrain

4. The shepherds at those tidings
   Rejoicèd much in mind,
   And left their flocks a-feeding,
   In tempest, storm, and wind,
   And went to Bethlehem straightway
   This blessèd babe to find:
   Refrain

5. But when to Bethlehem they came,
   Whereat this infant lay
   They found him in a manger,
   Where oxen feed on hay;
   His mother Mary kneeling,
   Unto the Lord did pray:
   Refrain

6. Now to the Lord sing praises,
   All you within this place,
   And with true love and brotherhood
   Each other now embrace;
   This holy tide of Christmas
   All others doth deface:
   Refrain

Good Christian Men, Rejoice

German

Ox and ass be - fore Him bow,

He is in the man - ger now;

Christ is born to - day!

Christ is born to - day!

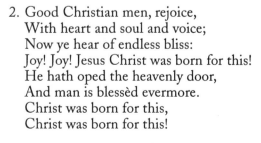

2. Good Christian men, rejoice,
   With heart and soul and voice;
   Now ye hear of endless bliss:
   Joy! Joy! Jesus Christ was born for this!
   He hath oped the heavenly door,
   And man is blessèd evermore.
   Christ was born for this,
   Christ was born for this!

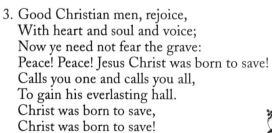

3. Good Christian men, rejoice,
   With heart and soul and voice;
   Now ye need not fear the grave:
   Peace! Peace! Jesus Christ was born to save!
   Calls you one and calls you all,
   To gain his everlasting hall.
   Christ was born to save,
   Christ was born to save!

O Come, O Come Emmanuel

French

1. O come, O come, Em-man - u - el, And ran - som cap - tive Is - ra - el, That mourns in lone - ly ex - ile here Un - til the Son of God _____ ap - pear.

Re - joice! Re - joice! Em - man - u - el shall come to thee, O Is - ra - el.

2. O come, thou dayspring, come and cheer
   Our spirits by thine advent here;
   Disperse the gloomy clouds of night
   And death's dark shadows put to flight.
   Refrain

3. O come, thou wisdom from on high
   And order all things, far and nigh;
   To us the path of knowledge show
   And cause us in her ways to go.
   Refrain

4. O come, desire of nations, bind
   All peoples in one heart and mind;
   Bid envy, strife, and quarrels cease;
   Fill the whole world with heaven's peace.
   Refrain

Fum, Fum, Fum

Spanish

Moderately

1. On this joy-ful Christ-mas Day, sing fum, fum, fum.

On this joy-ful Christ-mas Day, sing fum, fum, fum. For a

bles-sed Babe was born, Up-on this day at break of morn. In a

man-ger poor and low-ly, Lay the Son of God most ho-ly, fum, fum, fum!

2. Thanks to God for holidays, sing fum, fum, fum.
Thanks to God for holidays, sing fum, fum, fum.
Now we all our voices raise, And sing a song of grateful praise,
Celebrate in song and story, All the wonders of His glory,
Fum, fum, fum.

Joy to the World

Words by Isaac Watts
Music by George Frideric Handel

2. Joy to the world! The Savior reigns;
Let men their songs employ;
While fields and floods, rocks, hills and plains
Repeat the sounding joy,
Repeat the sounding joy,
Repeat, repeat the sounding joy.

3. He rules the world with truth and grace,
And makes the nations prove
The glories of His righteousness,
And wonders of His love,
And wonders of His love,
And wonders, wonders of His love.

We Wish You a Merry Christmas

English

Merrily

1. We wish you a Mer-ry Christ-mas, We wish you a Mer-ry Christ-mas; We wish you a Mer-ry Christ-mas, And a Hap-py New Year!

Refrain

Good ti-dings to you, And all of your kin, Good ti-dings for Christ-mas, And a Hap-py New Year.

2. Oh, bring us some figgy pudding,
Oh, bring us some figgy pudding,
Oh, bring us some figgy pudding,
And bring it right here!
Refrain

3. We won't go until we get some,
We won't go until we get some,
We won't go until we get some,
So bring it right here.
Refrain

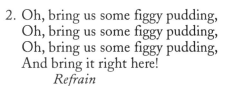

Everywhere, Everywhere, Christmas Tonight!

EVERYWHERE, everywhere, Christmas tonight!
Christmas in lands of the fir-tree and pine,
Christmas in lands of the palm-tree and vine,
Christmas where snow peaks stand solemn and white,
Christmas where cornfields stand sunny and bright.
Christmas where children are hopeful and gay,
Christmas where old men are patient and gray,
Christmas where peace, like a dove in his flight,
Broods o'er brave men in the thick of the fight;
Everywhere, everywhere, Christmas tonight!

PHILLIPS BROOKS

Oh, a Wonderful Pudding!

HALLO! A great deal of steam! The pudding was out of the copper. A smell like a washing-day! That was the cloth. A smell like an eating-house and a pastrycook's next door to each other, with a laundress's next door to that! That was the pudding! In half a minute Mrs. Cratchit entered—flushed, but smiling proudly—with the pudding, like a speckled cannon-ball, so hard and firm, blazing in half of half-a-quartern of ignited brandy, and bedight with Chrismas holly stuck onto the top.

Oh, a wonderful pudding! Bob Cratchit said, and calmly too, that he regarded it as the greatest success achieved by Mrs. Cratchit since their marriage. Mrs. Cratchit said that now the weight was off her mind, she would confess she had had her doubts about the quantity of flour. Everybody had something to say about it, but nobody said or thought it was at all a small pudding for a large family. It would have been flat heresy to do so. Any Cratchit would have blushed to hint at such a thing.

At last the dinner was all done, the cloth was cleared, the hearth swept, and the fire made up. The compound in the jug being tasted, and considered perfect, apples and oranges were put upon and table, and a shovel-full of chestnuts on the fire. Then all the Cratchit family drew round the hearth, in what Bob Cratchit called a circle, meaning half a one; and at Bob Cratchit's elbow stood the family display of glass. Two tumblers, and a custard-cup without a handle.

These held the hot stuff from the jug, however, as well as golden goblets would have done; and Bob served it out with beaming looks, while the chestnuts on the fire sputtered and cracked noisily. Then Bob proposed:

"A Merry Christmas to us all, my dears. God bless us!"

Which all the family re-echoed.

"God bless us every one!" said Tiny Tim, the last of all.

FROM *A CHRISTMAS CAROL* BY CHARLES DICKENS

Figgy Pudding

1¼ cups sifted flour
1 teaspoon baking soda
¼ teaspoon salt
1½ teaspoons pumpkin pie spice
½ cup finely chopped walnuts
½ cup finely chopped pecans
1 cup candied mixed fruits
¼ cup margarine
1 cup brown sugar
2 eggs
1 cup finely chopped dried figs
1 cup grated carrots
1 cup grated raw potatoes

Hard Sauce:
½ cup butter
3 tablespoons hot cream
1 teaspoon vanilla extract
½ teaspoon lemon extract
2 cups confectioners' sugar

1. Sift together the flour, baking soda, salt, and pumpkin pie spice. Add finely chopped nuts and candied fruits. In another bowl, blend the ¼ cup margarine, brown sugar, and eggs and then stir into dry ingredients. Add the figs, carrots, and potatoes and stir until thoroughly mixed.

2. Pour mixture into a greased 1½-quart mold. Fill two-thirds full and cover with a lid or foil. Place on a trivet or rack in a large pan with an inch of boiling water in it. Cover lightly and steam for 2 hours, adding additional water as it boils away.

3. To make hard sauce: Mix ingredients and beat until very creamy. Chill. Serve over the hot pudding.

Note: If you want to use a blender to chop the figs, place the figs in the blender and process on "Grate" to a paste. To chop by hand, first cover the whole figs with boiling water and allow to stand for 10 minutes. Cool and chop fine.

Serves 6 to 8.

The First Nowell

English

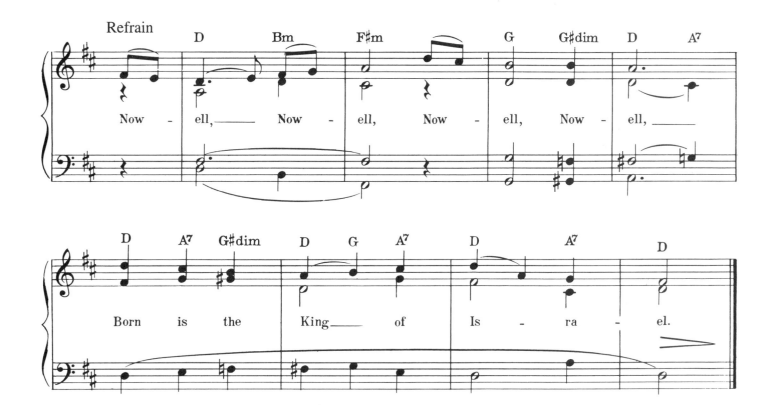

Refrain

Now-ell,___ Now-ell, Now-ell, Now-ell,___

Born is the King___ of Is - ra - el.

3. And by the light of that same star
   Three wise men came from country far;
   To seek for a king was their intent
   And to follow the star wheresoever it went.
   Refrain

4. This star drew nigh to the northwest;
   O'er Bethlehem it took its rest.
   And there it did both stop and stay
   Right over the place where Jesus lay.
   Refrain

5. Then entered in those wise men three
   Fell reverently upon their knee,
   And offered there in his presence
   Both gold and myrrh and frankincense.
   Refrain

6. Then let us all with one accord
   Sing praises to our heavenly Lord
   That hath made heaven and earth of naught
   And with his blood mankind hath brought.
   Refrain

Angels We Have Heard on High

French

1. An-gels we have heard on high, Sweet-ly sing-ing on the plain.
2. Shep-herds why this ju - bi-lee ? Why your joy-ful strains pro-long ?

And the moun-tains in re-ply Ech-o-ing their joy - ous strain:
What the glad-some ti - dings be Which in-spire your heav' - nly song ?

Refrain

Glo - - - - - - - - - - - - ri-a

in ex-cel-sius de - o. de - o.

3. Come to Bethlehem and see
   Him whose birth the angels sing;
   Come adore on bended knee
   Christ, the Lord, the newborn King.
   Refrain

4. See Him in a manger laid,
   Whom the choir of angels priase;
   Holy Spirit lend thine aid,
   While our hearts in love we raise.
   Refrain

Hark! the Herald Angels Sing

Words by Charles Wesley
Music by Felix Mendelssohn

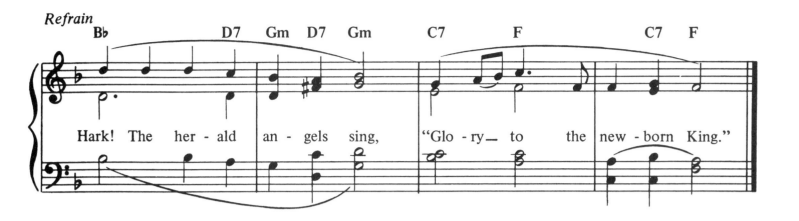

Refrain

Hark! The her-ald an-gels sing, "Glo-ry— to the new-born King."

2. Christ, by highest heaven adored;
Christ, the everlasting Lord;
Late in time behold Him come,
Offspring of the Virgin's womb.
Veiled in flesh the Godhead see;
Hail th'Incarnate Deity,
Pleased as man with man to dwell;
Jesus, our Emmanuel.
Refrain

3. Hail the heavenborn Prince of Peace!
Hail the Sun of Righteousness!
Light and life to all He brings,
Risen with healing in his wings;
Mild He lays his glory by,
Born that man no more may die,
Born to raise the sons of earth,
Born to give them second birth.
Refrain

Angels From the Realms of Glory

Words by James Montgomery
Music by Henry Smart

With spirit

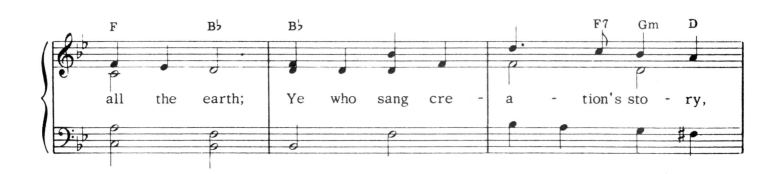

1. An - gels From The Realms Of Glo - ry, Wing your flight o'er

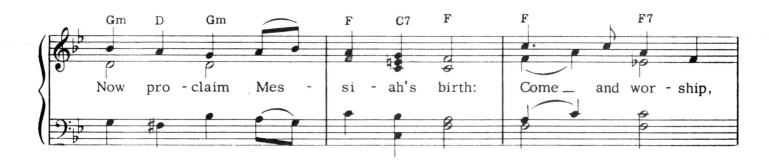

all the earth; Ye who sang cre - a - tion's sto - ry,

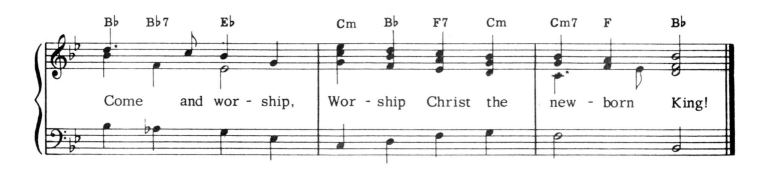

Now pro - claim Mes - si - ah's birth: Come __ and wor - ship,

Come and wor - ship, Wor - ship Christ the new - born King!

2. Shepherds, in the fields abiding,
   Watching o'er your flocks by night,
   God with man is now residing,
   Yonder shines the infant light:
   Come and worship, Come and worship,
   Worship Christ, the newborn King!

3. Sages, leave your contemplations,
   Brighter visions beam afar;
   Seek the great desire of nations;
   Ye have seen His natal star:
   Come and worship, Come and worship,
   Worship Christ, the newborn King!

Nowell! Nowell!

German

Majestically

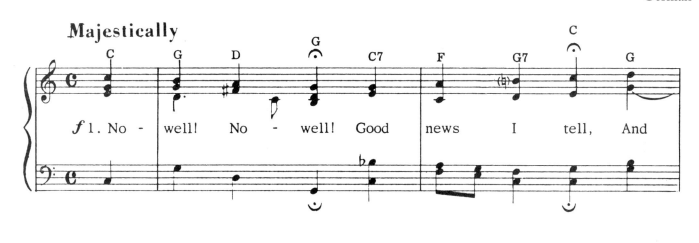

f 1. No - well! No - well! Good news I tell, And

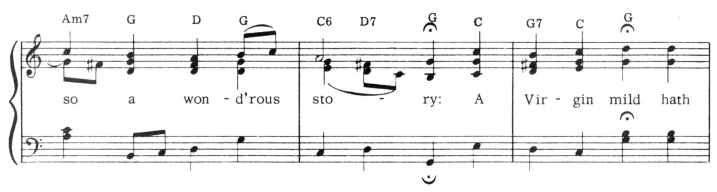

so a won - d'rous sto - ry: A Vir - gin mild hath

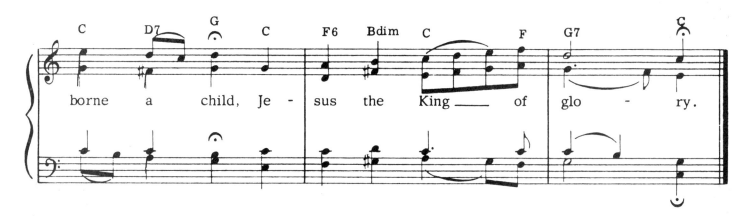

borne a child, Je - sus the King ___ of glo - ry.

2. Ave Marie! O well is Thee,
   Thou daughter born of Anna,
   Before that Son, that Holy One,
   Archangels sang Hosanna.

3. Then praise be sung and bells be rung,
   To greet this kindly stranger,
   Th'ancient of days, mankind to raise,
   Abhorreth not the manger.

And it came to pass in those days that there went out a decree from Cæsar Augustus, that all the world should be taxed.

And all went to be taxed, every one into his own city.

And Joseph also went up from Galilee, out of the city of Nazareth, into Judea, unto the city of David, which is called Bethlehem, (because he was of the house and lineage of David,)

To be taxed with Mary his espoused wife, being great with child.

And so it was, that, while they were there, the days were accomplished that she should be delivered.

And she brought forth her firstborn son, and wrapped him in swaddling clothes, and laid him in a manger; because there was no room for them in the inn.

And there were in the same country shepherds abiding in the field, keeping watch over their flock by night.

And, lo, the angel of the Lord came upon them, and the glory of the Lord shone round about them; and they were sore afraid.

And the angel said unto them, Fear not: for, behold, I bring you good tidings of great joy, which shall be to all people.

For unto you is born this day in the city of David a Saviour, which is Christ the Lord.

And this shall be a sign unto you; Ye shall find the babe wrapped in swaddling clothes, lying in a manger.

And suddenly there was with the angel a multitude of the heavenly host praising God, and saying,

Glory to God in the highest, and on earth peace, good will toward men.

Luke 2, 1–14

Scripture Cake

½ cup Deuteronomy 32:14
¾ cup Jeremiah 6:20
3½ tablespoons I Samuel 14:25
3 Jeremiah 17:11
2 cups Judges 15:1
¼ teaspoon Leviticus 2:13
1½ teaspoons Amos 4:5
1½ tablespoons II Chronicles 9:9
½ cup Judges 5:25
1 cup I Samuel 30:12
½ cup chopped Nahum 3:12
1 cup slivered Numbers 17:8
¼ cup sliced Numbers 17:8

Jeremiah 6:20

1. Preheat the oven to 325°F. Grease and flour a 9″×5″×2″ loaf pan.

2. Cream the Deuteronomy 32:14 with the Jeremiah 6:20 until light. Add ½ tablespoon of the I Samuel 14:25 and three Jeremiah 17:11, one at a time, beating well.

3. Sift the Judges 15:1 with the Leviticus 2:13, Amos 4:5, and Chronicles 9:9. Add the sifted mixture to the creamed mixture alternately with the Judges 5:25. Stir in the I Samuel 30:12, Nahum 3:12, and slivered Numbers 17:8. Pour the batter into the loaf pan and bake for 1 hour.

4. Turn the loaf out of the pan and allow to cool. Glaze with the remaining 3 tablespoons of I Samuel 14:25 and sprinkle with the sliced Numbers 17:8.

4. Turn the loaf out of the pan and allow to cool. Glaze with the remaining 3 tablespoons of honey and sprinkle with the sliced almonds.

3. Sift the flour with the salt, baking powder, and pumpkin pie spice. Add the sifted mixture to the creamed mixture alternately with the water. Stir in the raisins, figs, and slivered almonds. Pour the batter into the loaf pan and bake for 1 hour.

2. Cream the butter with the sugar until light. Add ¾ tablespoon of the honey and 3 eggs, one at a time, beating well.

1. Preheat the oven to 325°F. Grease and flour a 9″×5″×2″ loaf pan.

Sugar

¼ cup sliced almonds
1 cup slivered almonds
½ cup chopped figs
1 cup raisins
½ cup water
1½ tablespoons pumpkin pie spice (mixed spices)
1½ teaspoons baking powder (leaven)
¼ teaspoon salt
2 cups flour
3 eggs
3½ tablespoons honey
¾ cup sugar
½ cup butter

Key to the Scripture Cake

Rise Up, Shepherd, an' Follow

African-American Spiritual

fol - low. Leave your sheep and leave your lambs, Rise up, shep-herd, an' fol - low.

Leave your ewes an' leave your rams, Rise up, shep-herd, an' fol - low.

Shepherds! Shake Off Your Drowsy Sleep

Traditional

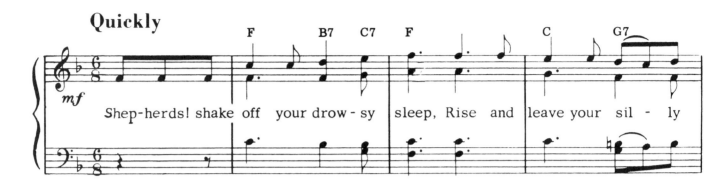

Shep-herds! shake off your drow-sy sleep, Rise and leave your sil - ly

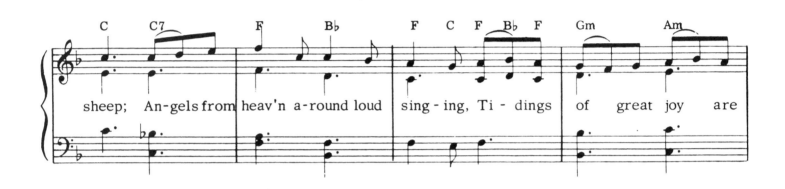

sheep; An-gels from heav'n a-round loud sing-ing, Ti - dings of great joy are

CHORUS

bring-ing Shep-herds! The cho - rus come and swell! Sing No- el O sing No - el.

2. Hark! Even now the bells ring 'round,
Listen to their merry sound;
Hark how the birds new songs are making!
As if winter's chains were breaking.
Chorus

3. See how the flow'rs all burst anew,
Thinking snow is summer dew;
See how the stars afresh are glowing,
All their brightest beams bestowing.
Chorus

4. Cometh at length the age of peace,
Strife and sorrow now shall cease;
Prophets foretold the wondrous story
Of this heav'n-born Prince of Glory.
Chorus

5. Shepherds, then up and quick away,
Seek the Babe ere break of day;
He is the hope of every nation,
All in Him shall find salvation.
Chorus

While Shepherds Watched Their Flocks

Words by Nahum Tate
Music by George Frideric Handel

1. While shepherds watched their flocks by night, All seated on the ground, The angel of the Lord came down, And glory shone around, And glory shone around.

2. "Fear not!" said He, for mighty dread
Had seized their troubled mind.
"Glad tidings of great joy I bring,
To you and all mankind,
To you and all mankind."

3. "To you, in David's town, this day
Is born of David's line
The Savior who is Christ the Lord,
And this shall be the sign,
And this shall be the sign."

4. "The heav'nly Babe you there shall find
To human view displayed,
All meanly wrapped in swathing band
And in a manger laid,
And in a manger laid."

5. "All glory be to God on high,
And to the earth be peace,
Good will henceforth from heav'n to men,
Begin and never cease,
Begin and never cease."

Run, Shepherds

Run, shepherds, run where Bethlehem blest appears.
We bring the best of news; be not dismayed:
A Saviour there is born more old than years,
Amidst heaven's rolling height this earth who stayed.
In a poor cottage inned, a virgin maid,
A weakling did him bear, who all upbears;
There is he poorly swaddled, in manger laid,
To whom too narrow swaddlings are our spheres:
Run shepherds, run, and solemnize his birth.
This is that night—no, day, grown great with bliss,
In which the power of Satan broken is:
In heaven be glory, peace unto the earth!
Thus singing, through the air the angels swarm,
And cope of stars re-echoèd the same.

WILLIAM DRUMMOND

Festive Shepherd's Pie

6 medium potatoes
3 tablespoons olive oil
1 medium onion, finely chopped
1 clove garlic, minced
1 ¼ pounds ground beef
2 bay leaves
1 tablespoon savory
½ cup chicken broth
1 cup canned tomatoes, crushed
1 tablespoon honey
1 apple, cored, peeled, and chopped
½ cup milk
2 tablespoons butter
Salt
Pepper
¼ cup peeled and diced carrots
½ cup peas
½ cup corn

1. Peel the potatoes and cut into pieces. Cover with water and bring to a boil. Allow to boil for 15 minutes, or until tender. Drain.

2. Heat the oil in a skillet and add the onion and garlic. When the onion is wilted, add the ground beef, bay leaves, and savory. Stir to mix ingredients and cook until the beef has browned. Drain off excess grease. Add the broth, tomatoes, honey, and apple. Cook until the broth evaporates, about 20 minutes. If too dry, add a little water. Take out and discard the bay leaves.

3. While the meat is cooking, heat the milk with the butter, and add to the potatoes, little by little, blending with a fork. Then beat with an electric mixer until they are fluffy. If you have a portable electric mixer, beat them in the pan so they stay hot. Add salt and pepper to taste.

4. In a small amount of water, boil the carrots for a few minutes, or until slightly tender. Add the peas and corn and continue boiling for a few more minutes until vegetables are slightly soft (do not overcook). (If you have a steamer basket, place the vegetables all together in the basket and steam until slightly tender.) Fold the vegetables into the potatoes and keep the mixture warm until your are ready to use it.

5. Pour the meat mixture into an 8-cup baking dish and cover with the mashed-potato-and-vegetable mixture. Place under the broiler for a few minutes to brown the top.

Serves 6 to 8.

Jolly Old Saint Nicholas

Traditional

2. When the clock is striking twelve,
   When I'm fast asleep,
   Down the chimney broad and black,
   With your pack you'll creep;
   All the stockings you will find
   Hanging in a row;
   Mine will be the shortest one,
   You'll be sure to know.

3. Johnny wants a pair of skates;
   Susy wants a dolly;
   Nellie wants a storybook,
   She thinks dolls are folly;
   As for me, my little brain
   Isn't very bright;
   Choose for me, old Santa Claus,
   What you think is right.

March of the Toys

Words by John Alan Haughton
Music by Victor Herbert

Toyland

Words by Glen McDonough
Music by Victor Herbert

When you're grown up, my dears —— And are as old as I —— You'll oft - en pon - der on the years That roll so swift - ly by, my dears, that roll so swift - ly by. —— And of the man - y lands —— You will have jour - neyed through —— You'll oft re - call The

D7 **Gm** **G7** **Em7(♭5)** **C7**

best of all, The land your child-hood knew____ Your child-hood knew.

rit.

Chorus
Tempo I
F6   **Am**   **Gm** **C7**   **F**   **B♭** **B♭m**

Toy - land! Toy - land! Lit - tle girl and boy - land, while you dwell with-

Am   **G7**   **C7**   **F6**   **Am**   **Gm** **C7**

in it____You are ev - er hap - py then. Child-hood's Joy - land, Mys-tic mer - ry

F   **Dm** **B♭m** **F** **D7**   **Gm** **C7**   **F**

Toy - land! Once you pass it's bor-ders you can ne'er_ re-turn a-gain.

Up on the Housetop

B.R. Hanby

1. Up on the house-top the rein-deer pause,
Out jumps good old San - ta Claus;
2. First comes the stock -ing the lit - tle Nell;
Oh, dear San - ta, fill it well;

Down through the chim-ney with lots of toys,
All for the lit -tle ones' Christ-mas joys:
Give her a dol - ly that laughs and cries,
One that will o-pen and shut its eyes:

Chorus

Ho, ho, ho, Who would -n't go? Ho, ho, ho, Who would-n't go?

Up on the house-top, click, click, click; Down through the chim-ney with good Saint Nick.

3. Next comes the stocking of little Will;
Oh, just see what a glorious fill;
Here is a hammer and lots of tacks,
Also a ball and a whip that cracks:
Chorus

St. Nicholas Cookies

Speculaas

½ cup shortening
¼ cup butter
1 cup light brown sugar, firmly packed
2 eggs
1 teaspoon vanilla
½ teaspoon almond extract
2½ cups all-purpose flour
1 teaspoon baking powder
½ teaspoon cinnamon
½ teaspoon nutmeg
½ teaspoon ground cloves
1 teaspoon salt
½ cup granulated sugar
Christmas cookie cutters

1. Allow shortening and butter to soften, then cream these together with the brown sugar in a large mixing bowl. Beat in the eggs, vanilla, and almond extract.

2. In a separate bowl, mix together the flour, baking powder, cinnamon, nutmeg, cloves, and salt.

3. Beat this dry mixture into the butter mixture until dough is well-blended.

4. Prehat oven to 400°F.

5. Roll dough ⅛-inch thick on a clean surface that has been dusted with flour. Cut into shapes, then sprinkle with granulated sugar. Place on ungreased baking sheets and bake for 6 to 8 minutes, or until light golden brown.

6. Allow to cool on the baking sheets. (Pierce before cooling, if desired, to hang as ornaments.)

Makes 4 dozen cookies.

The Night Before Christmas

TWAS THE NIGHT before Christmas, when all through the house
Not a creature was stirring, not even a mouse.
The stockings were hung by the chimney with care,
In hopes that St. Nicholas soon would be there.
The children were nestled all snug in their beds,
While visions of sugar plums danced in their heads;
And mamma in her kerchief, and I in my cap,
Had just settled our brains for a long winter's nap—
When out on the lawn there arose such a clatter
I sprang from my bed to see what was the matter.
Away to the window I flew like a flash,
Tore open the shutter, and threw up the sash.
The moon on the breast of the new fallen snow
Gave a luster of midday to objects below;
When what to my wondering eyes should appear
But a miniature sleigh and eight tiny reindeer,
With a little old driver, so lively and quick,
I knew in a moment it must be St. Nick!
More rapid than eagles his coursers they came,
And he whistled and shouted and called them by name.
"Now, Dasher! now, Dancer! now, Prancer and Vixen!
On, Comet! on, Cupid! on Donder and Blitzen!
To the top of the porch, to the top of the wall,
Now, dash away, dash away, dash away all!"
As dry leaves that before the wild hurricane fly,
When they meet with an obstacle mount to the sky,
So, up to the housetop the coursers they flew,
With a sleigh full of toys—and St. Nicholas, too.
And then, in a twinkling, I heard on the roof
The prancing and pawing of each little hoof.
As I drew in my head, and was turning around,
Down the chimney St. Nicholas came with a bound:
He was dressed all in fur from his head to his foot,
And his clothes were all tarnished with ashes and soot:

A bundle of toys he had flung on his back,
And he looked like a peddler just opening his pack.
His eyes, how they twinkled! his dimples, how merry!
His cheeks were like roses, his nose like a cherry;
His droll little mouth was drawn up like a bow,
And the beard on his chin was as white as the snow.
The stump of a pipe he held tight in his teeth,
And the smoke, it encircled his head like a wreath.
He had a broad face and a little round belly
That shook, when he laughed, like a bowl full of jelly.
He was chubby and plump—a right jolly old elf:
And I laughed when I saw him, in spite of myself;
A wink of his eye, and a twist of his head,
Soon gave me to know I had nothing to dread.
He spoke not a word, but went straight to his work,
And filled all the stocking: then turned with a jerk,
And laying his finger aside of his nose,
And giving a nod, up the chimney he rose.
He sprang to his sleigh, to his team gave a whistle,
And away they all flew like the down of a thistle.
But I heard him exclaim, ere they drove out of sight,
"Happy Christmas to all, and to all a good night!"

CLEMENT C. MOORE

Jingle Bells

James Pierpont

Chorus

Jin - gle bells! Jin - gle bells! Jin - gle all the

way! Oh, what fun it is to ride In a

1.
one - horse o - pen sleigh. Oh,

2.
one - horse o - pen sleigh!

Glad Christmas Bells

Traditional

Glad_ Christmas bells, your_ mu-sic tells, The_ sweet and pleasant sto—ry; How_ came to earth, in___ low-ly birth, The__ Lord of life and glo — ry.

2. No palace hall its ceiling tall
   His kingly head spread over,
   There only stood a stable rude
   The heav'nly babe to cover.

3. No raiment gay, as there He lay,
   Adorn'd the infant stranger;
   Poor, humble child of mother mild
   She laid Him in a manger.

4. But from afar, a splendid star
   The wise men westward turning;
   The livelong night saw pure and bright,
   Above His birthplace burning.

Ding Dong Merrily on High

French

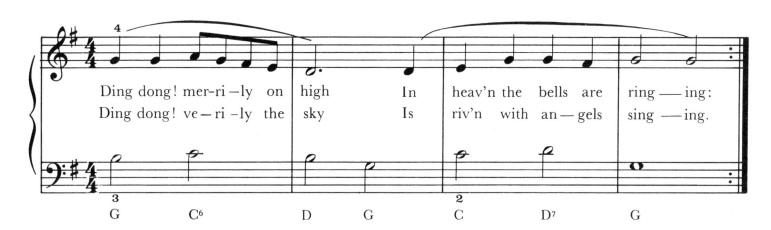

Ding dong! mer-ri-ly on high   In   heav'n the bells are   ring——ing:
Ding dong! ve-ri-ly the sky   Is   riv'n with an—gels   sing——ing.

G   C⁶   D   G   C   D⁷   G

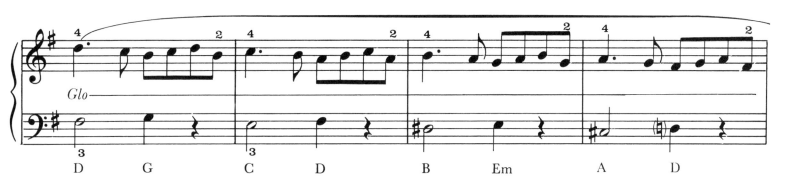

Glo——

D   G   C   D   B   Em   A   D

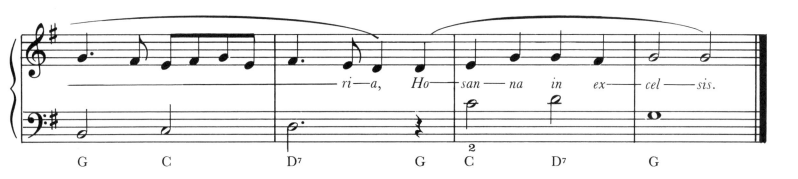

——ri—a, Ho-san——na in ex——cel——sis.

G   C   D⁷   G   C   D⁷   G

2. Praise Him! people far and near,
And join the angels' singing.
Ding dong, everywhere we hear
The Christmas bells a-ringing.
Refrain

3. Hear them ring this happy morn!
Our God a gift has given;
Ding dong, Jesus Christ is born!
A precious child from heaven.
Refrain

I Heard the Bells on Christmas Day

Words by Henry Wadsworth Longfellow

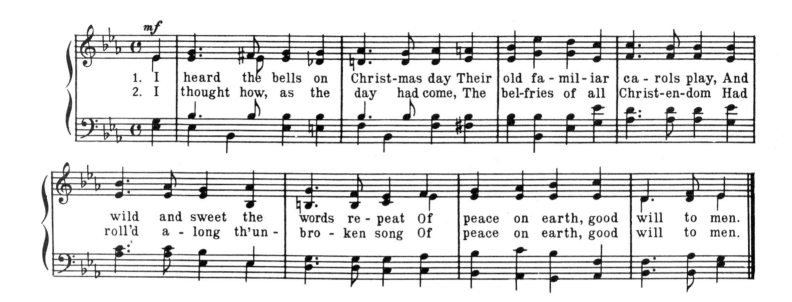

1. I heard the bells on Christ-mas day Their old fa - mil - iar ca - rols play, And
2. I thought how, as the day had come, The bel-fries of all Christ-en-dom Had

wild and sweet the words re - peat Of peace on earth, good will to men.
roll'd a - long th'un - bro - ken song Of peace on earth, good will to men.

3. Till, ringing, swinging on its way,
   The world revolved from night to day,
   A voice, a chime, a chant sublime
   Of peace on earth, good will to men.

4. Then from each black, accursèd mouth
   The cannon thundered in the South,
   And with the sound, the carols drowned
   Of peace on earth, good will to men.

5. It was as if an earthquake rent
   The hearth-stones of a continent,
   And made forlorn the households born
   Of peace on earth, good will to men.

6. And in despair I bowed my head;
   "There is no peace on earth," I said;
   "For hate is strong, and mocks the song
   Of peace on earth, good will to men."

7. Then pealed the bells more loud and deep:
   "God is not dead; nor doth He sleep!
   The wrong shall fail, the right prevail,
   With peace on earth, good will to men."

CHRISTMAS BELLS

Pat-a-Pan

French

1. Willie, bring your little drum; Robin, bring your fife and come; And be merry while you play, Tu-re-lu-re-lu, Pat-a-pat-a pan, Come be merry while you play, Let us make our Christmas gay!

2. When the men of olden days
   To the King of Kings gave praise,
   On the fife and drum did play,
   Tu-re-lu-re-lu,
   Pat-a-pat-a-pan,
   On the fife and drum did play,
   So their hearts were glad and gay!

3. God and man today become
   More in tune than fife and drum,
   So be merry while you play,
   Tu-re-lu-re-lu,
   Pat-a-pat-a-pan,
   So be merry while you play,
   Sing and dance this Christmas gay!

Il Est Né

He Is Born

French

The Boar's Head Carol

English

1. The boar's____ head in hand bear I, Bedecked with bays and rose-mar-y And I pray you, mas-ters,
be mer-ry *Quot es - tis in con - vi - vi - o.*
(Who-ev - er at the feast may be,

Refrain

Ca - put a - pri de - fe - ro, Re - dens lau - des Do - mi - no.
A boar's head I bear____ To give prais-es to the Lord.)

2. The boar's head as I understand
   Is the bravest dish in all the land,
   When thus bedecked with a gay garland
   Let us *servire cantico*.
   (Let us now serve it with a song.)
       Refrain

3. Our steward hath provided this
   In honor of the King of Bliss,
   Which on this day to be servèd is,
   In reginensi atrio.
   (All within this royal hall.)
       Refrain

Masters in This Hall

English

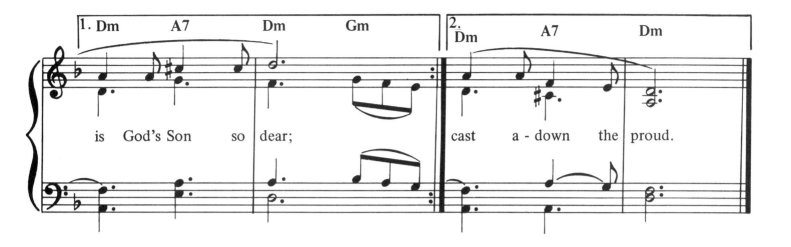

is God's Son so dear; cast a-down the proud.

2. Then to Bethl'em town
   We went two and two;
   In a sorry place
   We heard the oxen low:
   Refrain

3. Ox and ass Him know,
   Kneeling on their knee,
   Wond'rous joy had I
   This little babe to see:
   Refrain

Old Christmas Feasting

ALL YOU THAT to feasting and mirth are inclined,
Come here is good news for to pleasure your mind,
Old Christmas is come for to keep open house,
He scorns to be guilty of starving a mouse:
Then come, boys, and welcome for diet the chief,
Plum-pudding, goose, capon, minced pies, and roast beef.

The holly and ivy about the walls wind
And show that we ought to our neighbors be kind,
Inviting each other for pastime and sport,
And where we best fare, there we most do resort;
We fail not of victuals, and that of the chief,
Plum-pudding, goose, capon, minced pies, and roast beef.

All travellers, as they do pass on their way,
At gentlemen's halls are invited to stay,
Themselves to refresh, and their horses to rest,
Since that he must be Old Christmas's guest;
Nay, the poor shall not want, but have for relief,
Plum-pudding, goose, capon, minced pies, and roast beef.

ENGLISH CAROL

Roast Beef and Yorkshire Pudding

6-pound rolled rib or standing rib
¼ teaspoon ground black pepper
¼ teaspoon salt

Yorkshire Pudding:
1 cup flour
¼ teaspoon salt
1 cup milk
2 large eggs

1. Wash the roast and pat dry with paper towels or a clean cloth.

2. Season the roast with salt and pepper, then let it stand at room temperature for an hour.

3. Preheat the oven to 325°F.

4. Place roast on a rack in an open roasting pan (with rib-side down if a standing rib, and fatty side up if a rolled rib). Insert meat thermometer in the center of the roast.

5. Roast meat until thermometer reads 150°F. (approximately 3 hours for medium doneness).

6. Remove roast from oven and spoon the drippings into a 9″×9″ baking pan. Place baking pan in oven to warm.

7. In a bowl, mix flour, salt, milk, and eggs until well-blended.

8. Remove baking pan from oven and increase oven temperature to 425°F.

9. Pour pudding batter into baking pan and bake for 25 minutes. Then return the roast to the oven, and continue baking the pudding for 10 more minutes (or until the pudding is collapsed and crispy around the edges).

10. Cut the pudding into 3″ squares and serve with roast.

Serves 8 to 10.

Christmas Is Coming

English

If you have no penny,
A ha'penny will do,
If you have no ha'penny
Then God bless you,
If you have no ha'penny
Then God bless you.

Christmas Eve in Olden Times

On Christmas Eve the bells were rung;
On Christmas Eve the mass was sung:
That only night in all the year,
Saw the stoled priest the chalice rear.
The damsel donn'd her kirtle sheen;
The hall was dress'd with holly green;
Forth to the wood did merry-men go,
To gather in the mistletoe.
Then open'd wide the Baron's hall
To vassal, tenant, serf, and all;
Power laid his rod of rule aside,
And Ceremony doffed his pride.
The heir, with roses in his shoes,
That night might village partner choose.
The lord, underogating, share
The vulgar game of "post and pair."
All hail'd, with uncontroll'd delight,
And general voice, the happy night
That to the cottage, as the crown,
Brought tidings of salvation down!

The fire, with well-dried logs supplied,
Went roaring up the chimney wide;
The huge hall-table's oaken face,
Scrubb'd till it shone, the day to grace
Bore then upon its massive board
No mark to part the squire and lord.
Then was brought in the lusty brawn
By old blue-coated serving man;
Then the grim boar's-head frowned on high,
Crested with bays and rosemary.
Well can the green-garbed ranger tell
How, when, and where the monster fell;
What dogs before his death he tore,
And all the baiting of the boar.
The wassail round in good brown bowls,
Garnish'd with ribbons, blithely trowls.
There the huge sirloin reek'd; hard by
Plum-porridge stood, and Christmas-pye;
Nor fail'd old Scotland to produce,
At such high tide, her savoury goose.

Walter Scott

Christmas Dinner at the Cratchits'

Such a bustle ensued that you might have thought a goose the rarest of all birds; a feathered phenomenon, to which a black swan was a matter of course—and in truth it was something very like it in that house. Mrs. Cratchit made the gravy (ready beforehand in a little saucepan), hissing hot; Master Peter mashed the potatoes with incredible vigor; Miss Belinda sweetened up the apple sauce; Martha dusted the hot plates; Bob took Tiny Tim beside him in a tiny corner at the table; the two young Cratchits set chairs for everybody, not forgetting themselves, and mounting guard upon their posts, crammed spoons into their mouths, lest they should shriek for goose before their turn came to be helped. At last the dishes were set on, and grace was said. It was succeeded by a breathless pause, as Mrs. Cratchit, looking slowly all along the carving knife, prepared to plunge it in the breast; but when she did, and when the long expected gush of stuffing issued forth, one murmur of delight arouse all round the board, and even Tiny Tim, excited by the two young Cratchits, beat on the table with the handle of his knife, and feebly cried Hurrah!

There never was such a goose. Bob said he didn't believe there ever was such a goose cooked. Its tenderness and flavor, size and cheapness, were the themes of universal admiration. Eked out by the apple sauce and mashed potatoes, it was a sufficient dinner for the whole family; indeed, as Mrs. Cratchit said with great delight (surveying one small atom of a bone upon the dish) they hadn't ate it all at last! Yet every one had had enough, and the youngest Cratchits, in particular, were steeped in sage and onion to the eyebrows!

FROM *A Christmas Carol* by Charles Dickens

Roast Goose
With Chestnut Dressing

One 10-pound goose
Salt
3 medium onions, peeled and quartered
4 stalks celery, sliced thick
4 ounces prepared mustard

Chestnut Dressing:
2 cups cooked wild rice or long-grain rice
8 ounces chestnut purée
1 small onion, finely chopped
4 tablespoons butter
¼ cup chopped parsley
1 teaspoon dried basil
Salt
Pepper

1. Rinse and dry the goose. Sprinkle with salt inside and out. Remove any fat from the body cavity and fill the cavity with onions and celery. (These will help absorb the grease and add flavor, but should not be eaten because they will be quite greasy.) Puncture holes in the breast to allow fat to escape. Liberally spread the goose with mustard. Place the goose on a rack or on the splatter shield of a shallow roasting pan.

2. Loosely cover the goose with foil and roast at 350°F near the bottom of the oven, allowing 25 minutes per pound. After 1 hour, remove the goose and empty the grease from the pan. Replace the goose and again spread with mustard. Cover lightly with foil again. Remove the foil ½ hour before the goose is done.

3. To prepare the chestnut dressing: Place the ingredients for the chestnut dressing in a saucepan. Mix together and heat. Serve in a separate bowl.

Serves 6 to 8.

Dame Get Up and Bake Your Pies

English

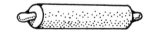

The Dame's Squab Pie

Pastry:
½ teaspoon salt
1½ cups all-purpose flour
½ cup shortening , chilled
2 tablespoons Worcestershire sauce
½ cup cold water

Filling:
2 squabs
Chicken stock
2 medium onions, chopped
2 tablespoons margarine
2 tablespoons flour
1 tablespoon powdered horseradish
    or 1½ tablespoons prepared horseradish
Dash pepper
6 small onions, peeled
6 radishes, trimmed and sliced
½ cup mushrooms, cleaned, trimmed, and sliced

1. Mix the salt into the flour in a large bowl. Cut the shortening into flour with 2 knives until it resembles coarse cornmeal. Put 2 tablespoons of Worcestershire sauce in the cold water and sprinkle the water over the flour, 1 tablespoon at a time, until the dough forms. Do not use more water than necessary. The dough should be soft and elastic. Roll the dough into a ball and chill for 30 minutes. Preheat the oven to 350°F. Roll out the dough and cut around a 2-quart casserole dish to form the top crust. Place dough on a greased cookie sheet and bake until golden brown.

2. Place the squabs in a deep saucepan. Add cold chicken stock just to cover. Bring to a boil over medium-low heat just until the surface begins to move. Skim off the broth. Cover and simmer over very low heat for 20 minutes or until the meat is tender. Cool to room temperature and remove the squabs. Reserve the broth and strain it. Remove the meat from the bones.

3. Sauté the chopped onions in the margarine. Blend in the 2 tablespoons flour. Season with the horseradish powder and a dash of pepper. Add the strained broth and stir over moderately low heat until thick and bubbly. Add the small onions, sliced radishes, and mushrooms. Stir in the squab meat. Pour into the casserole dish, place the pastry lid on top, and serve.

Serves 6 to 8.

Granny's Cake

CHRISTMAS is come and every hearth
Makes room to give him welcome now,
E'en Want will dry its tears in mirth
And crown him with a holly bough.

Though tramping 'neath a winter's sky
O'er snow track paths and rimy stiles,
The housewife sets her spinning by
And bids him welcome with her smiles.

Neighbors resume their annual cheer,
Wishing with smiles and spirits high,
Glad Christmas and a happy year
To every morning passerby.

Milk maids their Christmas journeys go,
Accompanied with favored swain,
And children pace the crumpling snow
To taste their granny's cake again.

FROM *THE SHEPHERD'S CALENDER* BY JOHN CLARKE

Christmas Fruitcake

1 cup light molasses
½ cup water
11 ounces raisins
11 ounces pitted prunes, diced
11 ounces pitted dates, diced
8 ounces packaged coconut, shredded
8 ounces banana chips
½ cup mixed candied fruit, diced finely
½ cup dried figs, diced
1½ cups pecans, chopped
1½ cups walnuts, chopped
2¼ cups all-purpose flour
1 cup plus 2 tablespoons unsalted butter
1½ cups sugar
6 eggs
1 tablespoon orange rind, grated
1 teaspoon salt
1½ teaspoons ground cinnamon
1¼ teaspoons ground nutmeg
¾ teaspoon ground allspice
½ teaspoon ground cloves
¼ teaspoon baking soda
½ cup orange juice
1 cup brandy

Note: Prepare fruitcakes one month in advance.

1. Stir the molasses and water together in a large saucepan over medium heat, and bring to a boil. Stir in the raisins, prunes, and dates, and return to a boil, stirring constantly. Stir in the raisins, prunes, and dates, and bring to a boil once again. Reduce the heat to low and simmer for 5 minutes. Remove from the heat, stir in the coconut, banana chips, and candied fruit. Set aside to cool.

2. Preheat the oven to 275°F. With 2 tablespoons of butter or shortening, grease two 9″ × 5″ loaf pans and line with greased wax paper.

3. Toss the pecans and walnuts with ¼ cup of flour.

4. Cream the butter until smooth and light. Gradually add the sugar, beating constantly. Beat in the eggs one at a time, then stir in the orange rind. Sift together the remaining flour, salt, cinnamon, nutmeg, allspice, cloves, and baking soda. Add this to the butter mixture alternately with orange juice. Stir in the fruit mixture and the nut-flour mixture. Pour into the prepared pans and bake for about 3 hours.

5. Store the fruitcakes in airtight containers for about a month, seasoning once a week with a few tablespoons of brandy.

Makes two 3½-pound cakes.

Here We Come A-Wassailing

English

2. We are not daily beggars
    That beg from door to door,
    But we are neighbors' children
    Whom you have seen before:
        Chorus

3. God bless the master of this house,
    Likewise the mistress, too;
    And all the little children
    That 'round the table go:
        Chorus

4. Good master and good mistress,
    While you're sitting by the fire,
    Pray think of us poor children
    Who are wandering in the mire:
        Chorus

"Christmas
for
Ever!"

Spiced Wassail

1 cup water
1 cup sugar
4 cinnamon sticks
1 teaspoon ground nutmeg
1 teaspoon ground ginger
10 whole cloves
2 cups orange juice
4 cups dry red wine
1 cup dry sherry
1 lemon, sliced

1. Boil water, sugar, and cinnamon sticks together for a few minutes until sugar is completely dissolved.

2. Reduce to low heat, add the remaining ingredients—keeping back half the lemon slices for a garnish. Simmer for 12 minutes.

3. Remove and discard cinnamon sticks, cloves, and lemon slices. Garnish with remaining orange slices and serve hot.

Serves 10 to 12.

Tangy Grape Punch

4 cups unsweetened grape juice
1½ cups superfine sugar
2 cups fresh-squeezed lemon juice
2 cups orange juice
2 quarts chilled ginger ale

1. Gradually add the grape juice to the sugar. Stir until dissolved.

2. Add lemon and orange juices. Stir and chill.

3. Pour over ice cubes placed in a 2-gallon punch bowl. Add ginger ale and stir.

Serves 12 to 14.

Gather Around the Christmas Tree

Words and music by J.H. Hopkins

Bright

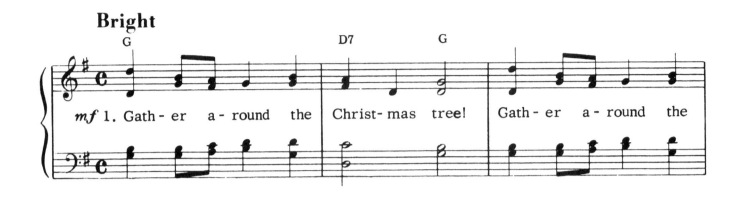

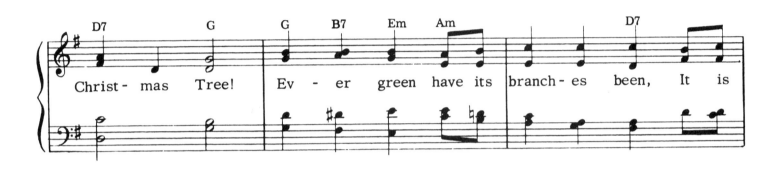

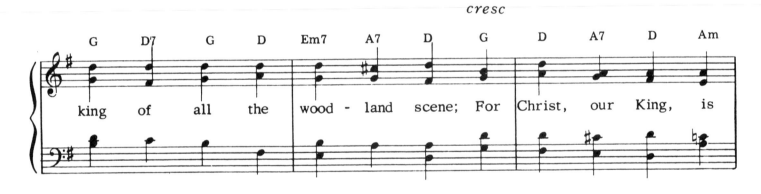

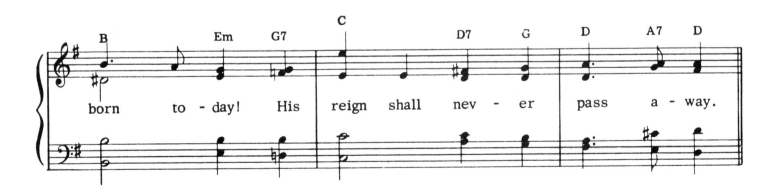

CHORUS

ff

Ho - san - na, Ho - san - na, Ho - san - na in the high - est.

2. Gather around the Christmas tree!
   Gather around the Christmas tree!
   Once the pride of the mountain side,
   Now cut down to grace our Christmastide:
   For Christ from heav'n to earth come down,
   To gain, through death, a noble crown.
   Chorus

3. Gather around the Christmas tree!
   Gather around the Christmas tree!
   Ev'ry bough bears a burden now,
   They are gifts of love for us, we trow:
   For Christ is born, His love to show,
   And give good gifts to me below.
   Chorus

O Christmas Tree

German

Moderately

1. O Christ-mas tree, O Christ-mas tree, How true you stand un - chang - ing. O

Christ-mas tree, O Christ-mas tree, How true you stand un - chang - ing. Your

boughs so green in sum-mer-time, Re - main so green in win-ter-time. O

Christ-mas tree, O Christ-mas tree, How true you stand un - chang - ing.

2. O Christmas tree, O Christmas tree,
Thy message is enduring;
O Christmas tree, O Christmas tree,
Thy message is enduring.
So long ago in Bethlehem
Was born the Savior of all men;
O Christmas tree, O Christmas tree,
Thy message is enduring.

3. O Christmas tree, O Christmas tree,
Thy faith is so unchanging;
O Christmas tree, O Christmas tree,
Thy faith is so unchanging.
A symbol sent from God above,
Proclaiming Him the Lord of Love;
O Christmas tree, O Christmas tree,
Thy faith is so unchanging!

A Pretty German Toy

I HAVE BEEN looking on, this evening, at a merry company of children assembled round that pretty German toy, a Christmas Tree. The tree was planted in the middle of a great round table, and towered high above their heads. It was brilliantly lighted by a multitude of little tapers; and everywhere sparkled and glittered with bright objects. There were rosy-cheeked dolls, hiding behind the green leaves; and there were real watches (with movable hands, at least, and an endless capacity of being wound up) dangling from innumerable twigs; there were French-polished tables, chairs, bedsteads, wardrobes, eight-day clocks, and various other articles of domestic furniture (wonderfully made, in tin, at Wolverhampton), perched among the boughs, as if in preparation for some fairy housekeeping; there were jolly, broad-faced little men, much more agreeable in appearance than many real men—and no wonder, for their heads took off, and showed them to be full of sugar-plums; there were fiddles and drums; there were tambourines, books, work-boxes, paint-boxes, sweetmeat boxes, peep-show boxes, and all kinds of boxes; there were trinkets for the elder girls, far brighter than any grown-up gold and jewels; there were baskets and pincushions in all devices; there were guns, swords, and banners; there were witches standing in enchanted rings of pasteboard, to tell fortunes; there were teetotums, humming-tops, needle-cases, pen-wipers, smelling-bottles, conversation-cards, bouquet-holders; real fruit, made artificially dazzling with gold leaf; imitation apples, pears, and walnuts, crammed with surprises; in short, as a pretty child, before me, delightedly whispered to another pretty child, her bosom friend, "There was everything, and more."

FROM *CHRISTMAS STORIES* BY CHARLES DICKENS

The Fir Tree

OUT IN THE FOREST stood a pretty little Fir Tree. It had a good place; it could have sunlight, air there was in plenty, and all around grew many larger comrades—pines as well as firs. But the little Fir Tree wished ardently to become greater. It did not care for the warm sun and the fresh air; it took no notice of the peasant children, who went about talking together, when they had come out to look for strawberries and raspberries. Often they came with a whole potful, or had strung berries on a straw; then they would sit down by the little Fir Tree and say, "How pretty and small that one is!" and the Fir Tree did not like to hear that at all.

Next year he had grown a great joint, and the following year he was longer still, for in fir trees one can always tell by the number of rings they have how many years they have been growing.

"Oh, if I were only as great a tree as the others!" sighed the littleFir. "Then I would spread my branches far around and look out from my crown into the wide world. The birds would then build nests in my boughs, and when the wind blew I could nod just as grandly as the others yonder."

He took no pleasure in the sunshine, in the birds, and in the red clouds that went sailing over him morning and evening.

When it was winter, the snow lay all around, white and sparkling, a hare would often come jumping along, and spring right over the little Fir Tree. Oh! This made him so angry. But two winters went by, and when the third came the little Tree had grown so tall that the hare was obliged to run around it. Oh! To grow, to grow, and become old; that's the only fine thing in the world, thought the Tree.

In the autumn woodcutters always came and felled a few of the largest trees; that was done this year, too, and the little Fir Tree, that was now quite well grown, shuddered with fear, for the great stately trees fell to the ground with a crash, and their branches were cut off, so that the trees looked quite naked, long, and slender—they could hardly be recognized. But then they were laid upon wagons, and horses dragged them away out of the wood. Where were they going? What destiny awaited them?

In the spring when the Swallows and the Stork came, the Tree asked them, "Do you know where they were taken? Did you not meet them?"

The Swallows knew nothing about it, but the Stork looked thoughtful, nodded his head, and said, "Yes, I think so. I met many new ships when I flew out of Egypt; on the ships were stately masts; I fancy these were the tress. They smelled like fir. I can assure you they're stately—very stately."

"Oh, that I were only big enough to go over the sea! What kind of thing is this sea, and how does it look?"

"It would take too long to explain all that," said the Stork, and he went away.

"Rejoice in thy youth," said the Sunbeams; "rejoice in they fresh growth, and in the young life that is within thee."

And the Wind kissed the Tree, and the Dew wept tears upon it; but the Fir Tree did not understand about that.

When Christmastime approached, quite young trees were felled, sometimes trees which were neither so old nor so large as this Fir Tree, that never rested, but always wanted to go away. These young trees, which were always the most beautiful, kept all their branches; they were put upon wagons, and horses dragged them away out of the wood.

"Where are they all going?" asked the Fir Tree. "They are not greater than I—indeed, one of them was much smaller. Why do they keep all their branches? Whither are they taken?"

"We know that! We know that!" chirped the Sparrows. "Yonder in the town we looked in at the windows. We know where they go. Oh! They are dressed up in the greatest pomp and splendor that can be imagined. We have looked in at the windows, and have perceived that they are planted in the middle of a warm room, and adorned with the most beautiful things—gilt apples, honey cakes, playthings, and many hundreds of candles."

"And then?" asked the Fir Tree, and trembled through all its branches. "And then? What happens then?"

"Why, we have not seen anything more. But it is incomparable."

"Perhaps I may be destined to tread this glorious path one day?" cried the Fir Tree rejoicingly. "That is even better than traveling across the sea. How painfully I long for it! If it were only Christmas now! Now I am great and grown up, like the rest who were led away last year. Oh, if I were only on the carriage! If I were only in the warm room, among all the pomp and splendor! And then? Yes, then something even better will come, something far more charming, or else why should they adorn me so? There must be something grander, something greater still to come; but what? Oh! I'm suffering. I'm longing! I don't know myself what is the matter with me!"

"Rejoice in us," said the Air and Sunshine. "Rejoice in thy fresh youth here in the woodland."

But the Fir Tree did not rejoice at all, but it grew and grew; winter and summer it stood there, green, dark green. The people who saw it said, "That's a handsome tree!" and at Christmastime it was felled before any of the others. The axe cut deep into its marrow, and the Tree fell to the ground with a sigh; it felt a pain, a sensation of faintness, and could not think at all of happiness, for it was sad at parting from its home, from the place where it had grown up; it knew that it should never again see the dear old companions, the little bushes and flowers all around—perhaps not even the birds. The parting was not at all agreeable.

The Tree only came to itself when it was unloaded in the yard, with other trees, and heard a man say, "This one is famous; we want only this one!"

Now two servants came in gay liveries and carried the Fir Tree into a large, beautiful salon. All around the walls hung pictures, and by the great stove stood large Chinese vases with lions on the covers; there were rocking chairs, silken sofas, great tables covered with picture books, and toys worth a hundred times a hundred dollars, at least the children said so. And the Fir Tree was put into a great tub filled with sand; but no one could see that it was a tub, for it was hung round with green cloth, and stood on a large, many-colored carpet. Oh, how the Tree trembled! What was to happen now? The servants, and the young ladies also, decked it out. On one branch they hung little nets, cut out of colored paper; every net was filled with sweetmeats; golden apples and walnuts hung down, as if they grew there, and more than a hundred little candles, red, white, and blue, were fastened to the different boughs. Dolls that looked exactly like real people—the Tree had never seen such before—swung among the foliage, and high on the summit of the Tree was fixed a tinsel star. It was splendid, particularly splendid.

"This evening," said all, "This evening it will shine."

Oh, thought the Tree that it were evening already! Oh, that the lights may soon be lit up! When may that be done? Will the Sparrows fly against the panes? Shall I grow fast here, and stand adorned in summer and winter? Yes, he did not guess badly. But he had a complete backache from mere longing, and backache is just as bad for a tree as a headache for a person.

At last the candles were lighted. What a brilliance, what a splendor! The Tree trembled so in all its branches that one of the candles set fire to a green twig, and it was scorched.

"Heaven preserve us!" cried the young ladies; and they hastily put the fire out.

Now the Tree might not even tremble. Oh, that was terrible! It was so afraid of setting fire to some of its ornaments, and it was quite bewildered with all the brilliance. And now the folding doors were thrown wide open, and a number of children rushed in as if they would have overturned the whole Tree; the older people followed more deliberately. The little ones stood quite silent, but only for a minute; then they shouted till the room rang; they danced gleefully round the Tree, and one present after another was plucked from it.

What are they about? thought the Tree. What's going to be done?

And the candles burned down to the twigs, and as they burned down they were extinguished, and then the children received permission to plunder the Tree. Oh! They rushed in upon it, so that ever branch cracked again: if it had not been fastened by the top and by the golden star to the ceiling, it would have fallen down. The children danced about with their pretty toys. No one looked at the Tree except one old man, who came up and peeped among the branches, but only to see if a fig or an apple had not been forgotten.

"A story! A story!" shouted the children; and they drew a little fat man toward the Tree; and he sat down just beneath it—"for then we shall be in the greenwood," said he, "and the Tree may have the advantage of listening to my tale. But I can only tell one. Will you hear the story of Ivede-Avede, or of Klumpey-Dumpey, who fell downstairs, and still was raised up to honor and married the princess?"

"Ivede-Avede!" cried some. "Klumpey-Dumpey!" cried others, and there was a great crying and shouting. Only the Fir Tree was quite silent, and thought, Shall I not be in it? Shall I have nothing to do in it? But he had been in the evening's amusement, and had done what was required of him.

And the fat man told about Klumpey-Dumpey, who fell downstairs and yet was raised to honor and married a princess. And the children clapped their hands and cried, "Tell another! Tell another!" and they wanted to hear about Ivede-Avede; but they only got the story of Klumpey-Dumpey. The Fir Tree stood quite silent and thoughtful; never had the birds in the wood told such a story as that. Klumpey-Dumpey fell downstairs, and yet came to honor and married a princess!

Yes, so it happens in the world! thought the Fir Tree, and believed it must be true, because that was such a nice man who told it. Well, who can know? Perhaps I shall fall downstairs, too, and marry a princess! And it looked forward with pleasure to being adorned again, the next evening, with candles and toys, gold and fruit. Tomorrow I shall not tremble, it thought. I shall rejoice in all my splendor. Tomorrow I shall hear the story of Klumpey-Dumpey again, and perhaps that of Ivede-Avede, too.

And the Tree stood all night, quiet and thoughtful.

In the morning the servants and the chambermaid came in. Now my splendor will begin afresh, thought the Tree. But they dragged him out of the room and upstairs to the garret, and here they put him in a dark corner where no daylight shone. What's the meaning of this? thought the Tree. What am I to do here? What is to happen?

And he leaned against the wall, and thought, and thought. And he had time enough, for days and nights went by, and nobody came up; and when at length someone came, it was only to put some great boxes in a corner. Now the Tree stood quite hidden away, and the supposition is that it was quite forgotten.

Now it's winter outside, thought the Tree. The earth is hard and covered with snow, and people cannot plant me; therefore I suppose I'm to be sheltered here until spring comes. How considerate that is! How good people are! If it were only not so dark here, and so terribly solitary! Not even a little hare? That was pretty out there in the wood, when the snow lay thick and the hare sprang past; yes, even when he jumped over me; but then I did not like it. It is terribly lonely up here!

"Peep! Peep!" said a little Mouse, and crept forward, and then came another little one. They smelled at the Fir Tree and then slipped among the branches.

"It's horribly cold," said the two little Mice, "or else it would be comfortable here. Don't you think so, old Fir Tree?"

"I'm not old at all," said the Fir Tree. "There are many much older than I."

"Where do you come from?" asked the Mice. "And what do you know?" They were dreadfully inquisitive. "Tell us about the most beautiful spot on earth. Have you been there? Have you been in the storeroom, where cheeses lie on the shelves, and hams hang from the ceiling, where one dances on tallow candles, and goes in thin and comes out fat?"

"I don't know that," replied the Tree; "but I know the wood, where the sun shines and the birds sing."

And then it told all about its youth.

And the little Mice had never heard anything of the kind; and they listened and said, "What a number of things you have seen! How happy you must have been!"

"I?" replied the Fir Tree; and it thought about what it had told. "Yes, those were really quite happy times." But then he told of the Christmas Eve, when he had been hung with sweetmeats and candles.

"Oh!" said the little Mice. "How happy you have been, you old Fir Tree."

"I'm not old at all," said the Tree. "I only came out of the wood this winter. I'm only rather backward in my growth."

"What splendid stories you can tell! said the little Mice.

And the next night they came with four other little Mice, to hear what the Tree had to relate; and the more it said, the more clearly did it remember everything, and thought, Those were quite merry days! But they may come again. Klumpey-Dumpey fell downstairs, and yet he married a princess. Perhaps I shall marry a princess, too! And the Fir Tree thought of a pretty little Birch Tree that grew out in the forest; for the Fir Tree, that Birch was a real princess.

"Who's Klumpey-Dumpey?" asked the little Mice.

And then the Fir Tree told the whole story. It could remember every single word; and the little Mice were ready to leap to the very top of the Tree with pleasure. Next night a great many more Mice came, and on Sunday two Rats even appeared; but these thought the story was not pretty, and the little Mice were sorry for that, for now they also did not like it so much as before.

"Do you know only one story?" asked the Rats.

"Only that one," replied the Tree. "I heard that on the happiest evening of my life; I did not think then how happy I was."

"That's a very miserable story. Don't you know any about bacon and tallow candles—a store-room story?"

"No," said the Tree.

"Then we'd rather not hear you," said the Rats. And they went back to their own people.

The little Mice at last stayed away also; and then the Tree sighed and said, "It was very nice when they sat round me, the merry little Mice, and listened when I spoke to them. Now that's past, too. But I shall remember to be pleased when they take me out."

But when did that happen? Why, it was one morning that people came and rummaged in the garret; the boxes were put away, and the Tree brought out; they certainly threw him rather roughly on the floor, but a servant dragged him away at once to the stairs, where the daylight shone.

Now life is beginning again! thought the Tree.

It felt the fresh air and the first sunbeam, and now it was out in the courtyard. Everything passed so quickly that the Tree quite forgot to look at itself, there was so much to look at all round. The courtyard was close to a garden, and here everything was blooming; the roses hung fresh over the paling, the linden trees were in blossom, and the Swallows cried, "Quinze-wit! Quinze-wit! My husband's come!" But it was not the Fir Tree that they meant.

"Now I shall live!" said the Tree rejoicingly, and spread its branches far out; but, alas! They were all withered and yellow; and it lay in the corner among nettles and weeds. The tinsel star, still upon it, shone in the bright sunshine.

In the courtyard a couple of the merry children were playing who had danced round the tree at Christmastime and had rejoiced over it. One of the youngest ran up and tore off the golden star.

"Look what is sticking to the ugly old Fir Tree!" said the child, and he trod upon the branches till they cracked again under his boots.

And the Tree looked at all the blooming flowers and the splendor of the garden, and then looked at itself, and wished it had remained in the dark corner of the garret; it thought of its fresh youth in the wood, of the merry Christmas Eve, and of the little Mice which had listened so pleasantly to the story of Klumpey-Dumpey.

"Past! Past!" said the old Tree. "Had I but rejoiced when I could have done so! Past! Past!"

And the servant came and chopped the Tree into little pieces; a whole bundle lay there; it blazed brightly under the great brewing copper, and it sighed deeply, and each sigh was like a little shot; and the children who were at play there ran up and seated themselves at the fire, looked into it, and cried, "Puff! Puff!" But at each explosion, which was a deep sigh, the Tree thought of a summer day in the woods, or of a winter night there, when the stars beamed; he thought of Christmas Eve and of Klumpey-Dumpey, the only story he had ever heard or knew how to tell; and the Tree was burned.

The boys played in the garden, and the youngest had on his breast a golden star, which the Tree had worn on its happiest evening. Now that was past, and the Tree's life was past, and the story is past, too: past! past! And that's the way with all stories. HANS CHRISTIAN ANDERSEN

The Lighting of the Yule Log

The Yule log is perhaps the very oldest of winter holiday traditions, dating back to pre-Christian times. To celebrate the winter solstice, Druid priests would ceremoniously carry in and light a huge log which was kept burning until spring to help the sun return to the desolate land. This custom was adopted by Christians and practiced throughout Europe during Medieval times. Even today, the fireplace is an important focal point in homes and gathering places throughout the world at Christmastime.

> May the fire of this Yule log
> Warm us from the cold.
> May the hungry be fed,
> May the weary find rest,
> And may all people everywhere
> Enjoy Heaven's peace.

Medieval prayer

Christmas Yule Log
Bûche de Noël

1 package of round chocolate bisquits
1 cup heavy cream
1 teaspoon vanilla
1 teaspoon cocoa powder
1 tablespoon sugar (or confectioner's sugar)
½ cup grated dark semi-sweet chocolate

1. With an electric mixer, whip cream until it begins to thicken, as you gradually add vanilla, cocoa powder, and sugar. Whip until thick, not stiff.

2. Spread whipped cream between bisquits and press them together, one at a time, to form a log.

3. When the log is finished, spread whipped cream over the top and sides.

4. Sprinkle top and sides of log with grated chocolate.

5. Chill until ready to serve.

The Holly and the Ivy

English

3. The holly bears a berry
   As red as any blood,
   And Mary bore sweet Jesus Christ
   To do poor sinners good.
       Refrain

4. The holly bears a prickle
   As sharp as any thorn,
   And Mary bore sweet Jesus Christ
   On Christmas Day in the morn.
       Refrain

5. The holly bears a bark
   As bitter as any gall,
   And Mary bore sweet Jesus Christ
   For to redeem us all.
       Refrain

6. The holly and the ivy,
   Now both are full well grown,
   Of all the trees that are in the wood
   The holly bears the crown.
       Refrain

Deck the Hall

Welsh

1. Deck the hall with boughs of hol-ly, Fa-la-la-la la, la la-la-la.

'Tis the sea-son to be jol-ly, Fa-la-la-la la, la la-la-la.

Don we now our gay ap-par-el, Fa-la-la, la-la-la, la-la-la.

Troll the an-cient Yule-tide car-ol, Fa-la-la-la la, la-la-la-la.

2. See the blazing Yule before us,
Fa-la-la-la-la, la-la-la-la.
Strike the harp and join the chorus,
Fa-la-la-la-la, la-la-la-la.
Follow me in merry measure,
Fa-la-la, la-la-la, la-la-la.
While I tell of Yuletide treasure,
Fa-la-la-la-la, la-la-la-la.

3. Fast away the old year passes,
Fa-la-la-la-la, la-la-la-la.
Hail the new, ye lads and lasses,
Fa-la-la-la-la, la-la-la-la.
Sing we joyous all together,
Fa-la-la, la-la-la, la-la-la.
Heedless of the wind and weather,
Fa-la-la-la-la, la-la-la-la.

Christ Was Born on Christmas Day

American

1. Christ was born on Christ-mas Day, Wreathe the hol - ly, twine the bay: *Christ - us na - tus ho - di - e,* The Babe, the Son, the Ho - ly One of Mar - y.

2. He is born to set us free, He is born, our lord to be: *Ex Mar - i - a Vir - gin - e,* The God, the Lord, by all a - dored for - ev - er.

3. Let the bright red berries glow
   Everywhere in goodly show:
   Christus natus hodie
   The Babe, the Son, the Holy One of Mary.

4. Christian men, rejoice and sing
   'Tis the birthday of a king:
   Ex Maria Virgine
   The God, the Lord, by all adored forever.

Under the Holly Bough

YE WHO HAVE scorn'd each other
Or injured friend or brother,
    In this fast fading year;
Ye who, by word or deed,
Have made a kind heart bleed,
    Come gather here.
Let sinn'd against and sinning,
Forget their strife's beginning;
Be links no longer broken,
Be sweet forgiveness spoken,
    Under the holly bough.

Ye who have lov'd each other,
Sister and friend and brother,
    In this fast fading year:
Mother, and sire, and child,
Young man and maiden mild,
    Come gather here;
And let your hearts grow fonder,
As memory shall ponder
    Each past unbroken vow.
Old loves and younger wooing,
Are sweet in the renewing,
    Under the holly bough.

Ye who have nourished sadness,
Estranged from hope and gladness,
    In this fast fading year.
Ye with o'er-burdened mind
Made aliens from your kind,
    Come gather here.
Let not the useless sorrow
Pursue you night and morrow,
    If e'er you hoped—hope now—
Take heart: uncloud your faces,
And join in our embraces
    Under the holly bough.

CHARLES MACKAY

December, month of holly, pine, and balsam,
Of berries red, of candles' mellow light;
Of home and fireside, laughter, happy faces,
Of peace that comes upon the holy night.

ANONYMOUS

Give me holly,
Bold and jolly,
Honest, prickly,
Shining holly.
Pluck me holly
Leaf and berry
For the day when
I make merry.

CHRISTINA ROSSETTI

The holly! the holly! oh, twine it with bay—
Come give the holly a song;
For it helps to drive stern winter away,
With his garment so sombre and long;
It peeps through the trees with its berries of red,
And its leaves of burnished green,
When the flowers and fruits have long been dead,
And not even the daisy is seen.
Then sing to the holly, the Christmas holly,
That hangs over peasant and king;
While we laugh and carouse 'neath its glittering boughs,
To the Christmas holly we'll sing.

ELIZA COOK

Under the Mistletoe

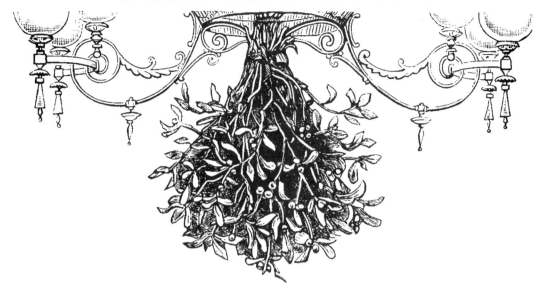

WHEN WINTER NIGHTS grow long,
And winds without blow cold,
We sit in a ring round the warm wood-fire,
And listen to stories old!
And we try to look grave (as maids should be),
When the men bring in boughs of the laurel tree.
    Oh the laurel, the evergreen tree!
    The poets have laurels—and why not we?

How pleasant when night falls down,
And hides the wintry sun,
To see them come in to the blazing fire,
And know that their work is done;
Whilst many bring in, with a laugh or rhyme,
Green branches of holly for Christmas time!
    O the holly, the bright green holly!
    It tells (like a tongue) that the times are jolly!

Sometimes—in *our* grave house
Observe this happeneth not—
But at times, the evergreen laurel boughs,
And the holly are all forgot!
And then! what then? Why the men laugh low,
And hang up a branch of—the mistletoe!
    Oh, brave is the laurel! and brave is the holly!
    But the mistletoe banisheth melancholy!
Ah, nobody knows, nor ever *shall* know,
What is done under the mistletoe!

FROM *RECOLLECTIONS OF OLD CHRISTMAS* BY BARRY CORNWALL

Lo, How a Rose E'er Blooming

Michael Praetorius

1. Lo, how a rose e'er bloom - ing, From ten - der root has sprung. To all the world be - stow - ing What men of old have sung. There bloomed a love - ly flow'r Though win - ter's cold was blow - ing, and mid - night was the hour.

2. Lo, how a rose came spring - ing, I - sa - iah did pro - claim; While all the heav'ns were sing - ing What The rose by Mar - y came. Through God's al - might - y pow'r The world sal - va - tion bring - ing, Though mid - night was the hour.

The Rose of Sharon

Go, pretty child, and bear this flower
Unto thy little Savior;
And tell Him, by that bud now blown,
He is the Rose of Sharon known.
When thou hast said so, stick it there
Upon his bib or stomacher;
And tell Him, for good handsel too,
That thou hast brought a whistle new,
Made of a clean straight oaten reed,
To charm his cries at time of need.
Tell Him, for coral, thou hast none,
But if thou hadst, He should have one;
But poor thou art, and known to be
Even as moneyless as He.
Lastly, if thou canst win a kiss
From those melifluous lips of His,
Then never take a second on
To spoil the first impression.

ROBERT HERRICK

Christmas Rosette Cake

3¼ cups cake flour
1 tablespoon plus 1½ teaspoons baking powder
2½ cups sugar
¾ teaspoon salt
¾ cup soft margarine
6 egg yolks
1 cup milk
1½ teaspoons rose water
6 egg whites

White Frosting:
1 cup sugar
⅓ cup water
¼ teaspoon cream of tartar
Dash of salt
2 egg whites, unbeaten
1 teaspoon rose water

Icing for Rosette Decorations:
1 pound confectioners' sugar (3½ cups), sifted
½ teaspoon cream of tartar
3 egg whites
1 teaspoon rose water
Few drops red food coloring

1. Preheat the oven to 350°F. Sift together the cake flour, baking powder, sugar, and salt. (If you are using self-rising flour, omit the baking powder and salt.) Add the margarine, egg yolks, ½ cup of the milk, and the rose water. Mix at medium speed until blended. Add the remaining ½ cup milk and the egg whites and beat at high speed until well mixed and a batter is formed.

2. Grease and flour one 9″ cake pan, one 8″ cake pan, and one 6″ cake pan. Pour batter into pans. Spread the batter in the pans so that there is less batter in the center than on the sides. Fill each pan only half to two-thirds full (this batter rises considerably). Bake for 30 to 35 minutes. Check the pans at 30 minutes: a toothpick inserted through the center of the cake should come out clean. The large pans will take 35 minutes. (Be sure the cake pans are not touching in the oven. If you do not bake all the pans at one time, cover the remaining pan with a damp towel.)

3. To make the frosting: Boil the sugar, water, cream of tartar, and salt until the sugar is dissolved. Add the resulting syrup very slowly to 2 unbeaten egg whites, while beating at high speed constantly for at least 7 minutes, or until the mixture reaches the consistency of a frosting. Add the rose water near the end of the beating. Use this frosting to fill and frost the cake.

4. To make icing for the fancy rosette decorations shown in the illustration, sift together the sugar and cream of tartar. Add egg whites and beat at high speed for 7 to 10 minutes. Add rose water and food coloring and beat until thick.

Serves 12 to 20.

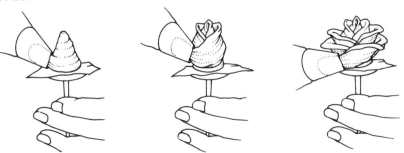

Pipe cone onto waxed paper.   *Pipe on overlapping petals.*

Sparkling Rose Water

1 apple, cored, peeled, and sliced
¼ teaspoon rose water
⅛ teaspoon red food coloring
4 cups carbonated water
ice cubes

1. Place the apple slices, rose water, and food coloring in blender.

2. Add 2 cups of the carbonated water and process for a few seconds, or until the apple is pulverized.

3. Stir in the remaining 2 cups of carbonated water and serve over ice.

Serves 4.

The Cherry Tree Carol

English

Gently

When Jos-eph was an old man, An old man was he, He
mar - ried Vir-gin Mar - y, The Queen of Ga-li-lee, He
mar - ried Vir-gin Mar - y, The Queen of Ga-li-lee.

2. When Joseph and Mary walked through an orchard green,
   There were berries and cherries as thick as might be seen,
   There were berries and cherries as thick as might be seen.

3. And Mary spoke to Joseph, so meek and so mild:
   "Joseph, gather me some cherries for I am with child,"
   "Joseph, gather me some cherries for I am with child."

4. And Joseph flew in anger, in anger flew he:
   "Let the father of the baby gather cherries for thee,"
   "Let the father of the baby gather cherries for thee."

5. The up spoke baby Jesus from in Mary's womb:
   "Bend down the tallest tree that my mother might have some,"
   "Bend down the tallest tree that my mother might have some."

6. And bent down the tallest branch till it touchèd Mary's hand,
   Cried she, "Oh, look thou Joseph, I have cherries by command."
   Cried she, "Oh, look thou Joseph, I have cherries by command."

Christmas Cherry Cheesecake

2 tablespoons butter
½ cup pound-cake crumbs
½ cup heavy cream
16 ounces cream cheese
1 teaspoon vanilla
Grated rind of 1 lemon
Grated rind of 1 orange
½ cup sugar
3 eggs
½ pint sour cream
1 teaspoon almond extract
¼ cup sugar
Red and green maraschino cherries, for garnish

1. Butter a 9″ spingform pan liberally. Sprinkle in the pound-cake crumbs. Shake well to cover bottom and sides of pan.

2. Preheat the oven to 375°F.

3. Mix together the heavy cream, cream cheese, vanilla, lemon and orange rinds, ½ cup sugar—and the eggs, one at a time. If you use a mixer, set it on low speed. Pour the batter over the crumbs. Place the spingform pan in a pan of boiling water in the center of the oven. Bake for 20 minutes. Remove, and cool for 10 minutes.

4. Mix together the sour cream, almond extract, and ¼ cup sugar. Spread this mixture over the cooled mixture.

5. Cut the maraschino cherries in half, place in a colander, and rinse well (this will prevent their colors from running). Decorate the top layer of the cake with the cherries (you might try a wreath around the edge or a single-star ray pattern emanating from the middle). Increase the oven temperature to 475°F. and bake for 10 more minutes.

Yields one 9″ cheesecake.

Whence Comes This Rush of Wings?

French

Moderate

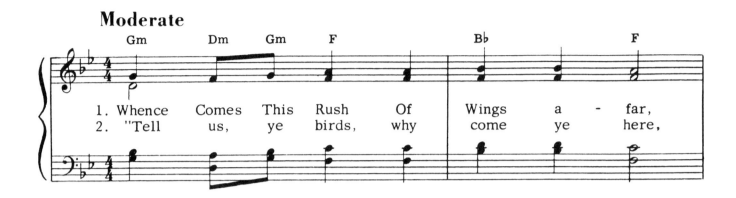

1. Whence Comes This Rush Of Wings a - far,
   Fol - low-ing straight the No - el star? Birds from the woods in
   won - d'rous flight, Beth - le - hem seek this ho - ly night.

2. "Tell us, ye birds, why come ye here,
   In - to this sta - ble poor and drear?" "Hast-'ning we seek the
   new - born King, And all the sweet - est mu - sic bring."

3. Hark, how the greenfinch bears his part!
   Philomel, too, with tender heart,
   Chants from her leafy dark retreat,
   Re, mi, fa, sol, in accents sweet.

4. Angels and shepherds, birds of the sky,
   Come where the Son of God doth lie;
   Christ on earth with man doth dwell,
   Join in the shout, "Noel, Noel!"

Christmas Greetings
From a Fairy to a Child

LADY DEAR, if Fairies may
 For a moment lay aside
Cunning tricks and elfish play,
'Tis at happy Christmas-tide.

We have heard the children say—
Gentle children, whom we love—
Long ago, on Christmas Day,
Came a message from above.

Still, as Christmas-tide comes round,
They remember it again—
Echo still the joyful sound,
"Peace on earth, good-will to men."

Yet the hearts must child-like be
Where such heavenly guests abide,
Unto children, in their glee,
All the year is Christmas-tide.

Thus, forgetting tricks and play
For a moment, Lady dear,
We would wish you, if we may,
Merry Christmas, glad New Year.

LEWIS CARROLL

The Bird of Dawning

SOME SAY that ever 'gainst that season comes
Wherein our Saviour's birth is celebrated,
The bird of dawning singeth all night long;
And then, they say, no spirit can walk abroad;
The nights are wholesome; then no planets
    strike,
No fairy takes, nor witch hath power to charm,
So hallow'd and so gracious is the time.

FROM *HAMLET* BY WILLIAM SHAKESPEARE

The Oriole's Nest

JUST AS THE moon was fading
    Amid her misty rings,
And every stocking was stuffed
    With childhood's precious things,

Old Kriss Kringle looked round,
    And saw on the elm-tree bough,
High-hung, an oriole's nest,
    Silent and empty now.

"Quite like a stocking," he laughed,
    "Pinned up there on the tree!
Little I thought the birds
    Expected a present from me!"

Then old Kriss Kringle, who loves
    A joke as well as the best,
Dropped a handful of flakes
    In the oriole's empty nest.

THOMAS BAILEY ALDRICH

I Saw Three Ships

English

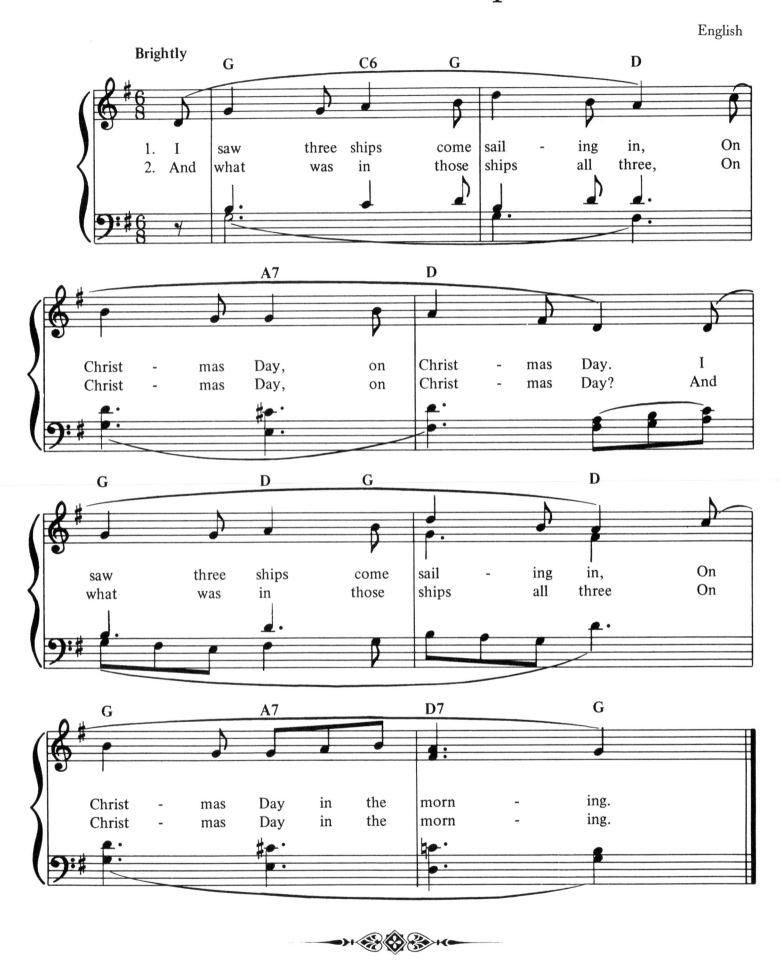

1. I saw three ships come sail - ing in, On
2. And what was in those ships all in three, On

Christ - mas Day, on Christ - mas Day. I
Christ - mas Day, on Christ - mas Day? And

saw three ships come sail - ing in, On
what was in those ships all in three On

Christ - mas Day in the morn - ing.
Christ - mas Day in the morn - ing.

3. Our Savior Christ and his lady,
   On Christmas Day, on Christmas Day,
   Our Savior Christ and his lady,
   On Christmas Day in the morning.

4. Pray, whither sailed those ships all three? *etc.*

5. O, they sailed into Bethlehem,

6. And all the bells on earth shall ring,

7. And all the angels in heav'n shall sing,

8. And all the souls on earth shall sing,

9. Then let us all rejoice amain!

Christmas Day at Sea

IN ALL MY TWENTY YEARS of wandering over the restless waters of the globe I can only remember one Christmas Day celebrated by a present given and received. It was, in my view, a proper live-sea transaction, no offering of Dead Sea fruit; and in its unexpectedness perhaps worth recording.

The daybreak of Christmas Day in the year 1879 was fine. The sun began to shine sometime about four o'clock over the somber expanse of the Southern Ocean in latitude 51; and shortly afterwards a sail was sighted ahead. The wind was light, but a heavy swell was running. Presently I wished a "Merry Christmas" to my captain. He looked sleepy, but amiable. I reported the distant sail to him and ventured the opinion that there was something wrong with her. He said, "Wrong?" in an incredulous tone. I pointed out that she had all her upper sails furled and that she was brought to the wind, which, in that region of the world, could not be accounted for on any other theory....

The captain, as is a captain's way, disappeared from the deck; and after a time our carpenter came up the poop ladder carrying an empty small wooden keg, of the sort in which certain ship's provisions are packed. I said, surprised, "What do you mean by lugging this thing up here, Chips?"

"Captain's orders, sir," he explained shortly.

I did not like to question him further, and so we only exchanged Christmas greetings and he went away. The next person to speak to me was the steward. He came running up the companion stairs. "Have you any old newspapers in your room, sir?"

We had left Sydney, N.S.W., eighteen days before. There were several old Sydney *Heralds, Telegraphs, Bulletins* in my cabin, besides a few home papers received by the last mail. "Why do you ask, steward?" I inquired naturally.

"The captain would like to have them," he said.

And even then I did not understand the inwardness of these eccentricities. I was only lost in astonishment at them. It was eight o'clock before we had closed with that ship, which, under her short canvas and heading nowhere in particular, seemed to be loafing aimlessly on the very threshold of the gloomy home of storms. But long before that hour I learned from the number of boats she carried that this nonchalant ship was a whaler. She had hoisted the Stars and Stripes at her peak, and her signal flags had already told us that her name was *Alaska*—two years out from New York—east from Honolulu—two hundred and fifteen days on the cruising ground.

We passed, sailing slowly, within a hundred yards of her; and just as our steward started ringing the breakfast bell, the captain and I held aloft, in good view of the figures watching us over her stern, the keg, properly headed up and containing, besides an enormous bundle of newspapers, two boxes of figs in honor of the day. We flung it far out over the rail. Instantly our ship, sliding down the slope of a high swell, left it far behind in our wake. On board the *Alaska* a man in a fur cap flourished an arm; another, a much bewhiskered person, ran forward suddenly. I never saw anything so ready and so smart as the way that whaler, rolling desperately all the time, lowered one of her boats. The Southern Ocean went on tossing the two ships like a juggler his gilt balls, and the microscopic white speck of the boat seemed to come into the game instantly, as if shot out from a catapult on the enormous and lonely stage. That Yankee whaler lost not a moment in picking up her Christmas present from the English wool clipper.

FROM *CHRISTMAS DAY AT SEA* BY JOSEPH CONRAD

Fig Danish

1 package dry yeast
½ cup lukewarm milk (105 to 115°F)
⅛ cup sugar
½ teaspoon salt
2 tablespoons soft margarine
1 egg
¼ teaspoon almond extract
¼ teaspoon mace
2 to 2½ cups all-purpose flour
½ cup finely chopped almonds
2 tablespoons melted butter
¼ cup superfine sugar

Fig Paste:
1 cup chopped figs
1 cup sugar
¼ cup orange juice

1. Stir the yeast into the warm milk; let sit. In a large bowl, mix the sugar, salt, margarine, egg, almond extract, and mace. Add the yeast mixture. Add 2 cups of flour, 1 cup at a time, until a soft, flexible dough forms. Knead well. If the dough is too sticky to handle, gradually add flour until it does not stick to the fingers. Form the dough into a ball and place in a greased bowl. Cover the bowl with plastic wrap and place in a warm, draft-free place for 1 hour, or until doubled.

2. While the dough is rising, chop the almonds in a food processor or blender until you have very fine crumbs.

3. To prepare fig paste: Combine the ingredients in a blender and blend to a paste.

4. When the dough has doubled, punch it down and roll it out as thinly as possible on a lightly floured board into a rectangle about 2 feet long and 8 inches wide. Brush the dough with the melted butter. Sprinkle with superfine sugar and cover with the fig paste. Sprinkle with the almond crumbs. Roll the dough from the long side like a jelly roll 2 feet long. Trim the ends and join them together to form a circle. Place on a greased baking sheet. With a pair of scissors, make cuts every 1½ inch, holding the scissors at a right angle to the dough. Cover with plastic wrap and let rise in a warm, draft-free place for about 1 hour.

5. Bake in a preheated 350°F oven for 20 to 25 minutes, or until golden brown. If you like a crisp crust, brush with melted butter before baking.

Serves 6 to 8.

Trim the ends

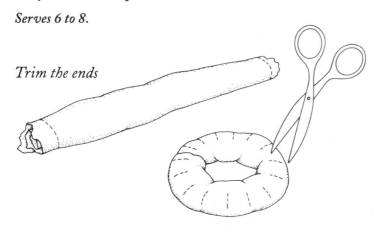

Form a circle and snip at 1½″ intervals

Silent Night

Words by Joseph Mohr
Music by Franz Gruber

2. Silent night! Holy night!
Shepherds quake at the sight!
Glories stream from heaven afar,
Heav'nly hosts sing Alleluia,
Christ, the Savior, is born!
Christ, the Savior, is born!

3. Silent night! Holy Night!
Sun of God, love's pure light,
Radiant beams from Thy holy face,
With the dawn of redeeming grace,
Jesus, Lord at Thy birth,
Jesus, Lord at Thy birth.

The Moon Shines Bright

English

1. The moon shines bright and the stars give light, A little before the day; Our mighty Lord, He looked on us, And bade us awake and pray!

2. Awake, awake, good people all, Awake, and you shall hear, The Lord our God died on the cross, For us He loved so dear.

O! Holy Night

Words by John Sullivan Dwight
Music by Adolphe Adam

It Came Upon a Midnight Clear

Words by Edmund H. Sears
Music by Richard S. Willis

2. Still through the cloven skies they come,
   With peaceful wings unfurled,
   And still their heav'nly music floats
   O'er all the weary world;
   Above its sad and lowly plain
   They bend on hovering wing
   And ever over its Babel sounds
   The blessèd angels sing.

3. Yet with the woes of sin and strife
   The world has suffered long;
   Beneath the angel-strain have rolled
   Two thousand years of wrong;
   And man, at war with man, hears not
   The love-song which they bring.
   O hush the noise, ye men of strife
   And hear the angels sing.

4. And ye, beneath life's crushing load,
   Whose forms are bending low,
   Who toil along the climbing way
   With weary steps and slow:
   Look up! for glad and golden hours
   Come swiftly on the wing;
   O rest beside the weary road
   And hear the angels sing.

5. For lo! the days are hastening on,
   By prophet bards foretold,
   When with the ever-circling years
   Comes round the Age of Gold.
   When peace shall over all the earth
   Its ancient splendors fling,
   And the whole world give back the song
   Which now the angels sing.

The Holy Night • 113

O Little Town of Bethlehem

Words by Phillips Brooks

1. O lit-tle town of Beth-le-hem! How still we see thee lie; A-bove thy deep and dream-less sleep The si-lent stars go by; Yet in thy dark streets shin-eth The ev-er last-ing light. The hopes and fears of all the years Are met in thee to-night.

2. For Christ is born of Mar-y, And gath-er to all a-bove. While mor-tals sleep, the an-gels keep Their watch of won-d'ring love. O morn-ing stars, to-geth-er Pro-claim the ho-ly birth! And prais-es sing to God the King, And peace to men on earth!

3. How silently, how silently,
   The wondrous gift is giv'n!
   So God imparts to human hearts
   The blessing of his heav'n.
   No ear may heart His coming,
   But in this world of sin,
   Where meek souls will receive Him still
   The dear Christ enters in.

4. O Holy child of Bethlehem!
   Descend to us, we pray;
   Cast out our sin, and enter in;
   Be born in us today.
   We hear the Christmas angels
   The great glad tidings tell;
   O come to us, abide with us,
   Our Lord Emmanuel.

The Star Song

TELL US, thou clear and heavenly tongue,
  Where is the Babe but lately sprung?
Lies he the lily-banks among?

Or say, if this new Birth of ours
Sleeps, laid within some ark of flowers,
Spangled with dew-light; thou canst clear
All doubts, and manifest the where.

Declare to us, bright star, if we shall seek
Him in the morning's blushing cheek,
Or search the beds of spices through,
To find him out?

Star.—No, this ye need not do;
But only come and see Him rest,
A princely babe, in's mother's breast.

ROBERT HERRICK

Ginger Nut Bread

1½ teaspoons vinegar
½ cup milk
1 teaspoon baking soda
1 egg, well beaten
⅔ cup butter
½ cup sugar
½ cup molasses
1 teaspoon ginger
1 teaspoon cinnamon
½ teaspoon ground cloves
1½ cups flour
1 cup chopped pecans
1 cup raisins

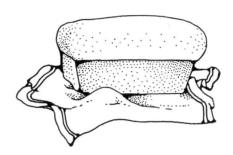

Whipped Cream Topping:
½ pint heavy cream
1 teaspoon vanilla
1 tablespoon confectioners' sugar (or regular sugar)

1. Preheat the oven to 325°F. Add the vinegar to the milk and let set 5 minutes to sour. Add the baking soda to the sour milk and stir. Let sit a few minutes and then add the well-beaten egg. Stir and allow to sit.

2. In a large bowl, cream the butter with the sugar. Add the molasses, ginger, cinnamon, and cloves and blend well. Add 1 cup of the flour and blend until smooth. Add the chopped pecans. Add the remaining ½ cup flour and blend well again. Add the raisins and stir until mixed. Scoop into a greased and floured 9″×5″×2½″ loaf pan and bake for 1 hour.

3. With an electric mixer, whip cream until it begins to thicken, while you gradually add the sugar and vanilla. Whip until thick but not stiff. Cut bread into thick slices, top with whipped cream, and serve.

Makes 1 loaf.

Milk and Honey Egg Nog

4 cups whole milk
2 cups heavy cream
½ cup honey
8 eggs
1 teaspoon vanilla extract
2 cups crushed ice
1 cup white rum (optional)
Nutmeg

1. Blend together the milk, cream, honey, eggs, vanilla, ice, and rum (if desired) until frothy.

2. Refrigerate until well chilled, sprinkle with nutmeg, and serve.

Away in a Manger

Music by James R. Murray
Words Traditional

2. The cattle are lowing, the baby awakes,
   But little Lord Jesus, no crying He makes.
   I love thee, Lord Jesus, look down from the sky,
   And stay by my cradle till morning is nigh.

3. Be near me Lord Jesus, I ask thee to stay
   Close by me forever, and love me, I pray.
   Bless all the dear children in thy tender care,
   And fit us for heaven to live with thee there.

Coventry Carol

English

Rocking

Czech

1. Lit - tle Je - sus, sweet - ly sleep, do not stir;
2. Mar - y's lit - tle ba - by sleep, sweet - ly sleep,

We will lend a coat of fur:
Sleep in com - fort, slum - ber deep:

We will rock you rock you, rock you, We will rock you, rock you, rock you,

See the fur to
We will serve you

keep you warm, Snug - ly round your ti - ny form.
all we can, Dar - ling, dar - ling lit - tle man.

Mary Had a Baby

African-American

Moderately

1. Mar-y had a ba-by, Oh Lord,_ Mar-y had a ba - by, Oh my_ Lord;

Mar-y had a ba-by, Oh Lord,_ The peo-ple keep a-com-ing and the train done gone.

2. What did she name him? Oh, Lord,
   What did she name him? Oh, my Lord;
   What did she name him? Oh, Lord,
   The people keep a-comin' and the train
   done gone.

3. She called him Jesus, *etc.*

4. Now where was he born?

5. Born in a stable,

6. Where did they lay him?

7. Laid him in a manger,

8. Who came to see him?

9. Shepherds came to see him,

10. The wise men kneeled before him,

11. King Herod tried to find him,

12. They went away to Egypt,

13. Angels watching over him,

Joseph Dearest, Joseph Mine

German

Slowly

p Jo - seph dear - est, Jo - seph mild, Help me rock my
lit - tle Child, God will give you your re - ward In
heav'n a - bove, The Son of Vir - gin Ma - ry.

2. Mary Dearest, Mary mine,
   I will help cradle this child of thine;
   God's own light on us both shall shine
   In paradise, as prays the Mother Mary.

3. Little man, and God indeed,
   Little and poor, thou'rt all we need;
   We will follow where thou dost lead,
   Thou little bird of love, the Son of Mary.

Bring a Torch, Jeanette Isabella

French

1. Bring a torch, Jean-ette Is-a-bel-la,
Un flam-beau, Jean-ette Is-a-bel-le,

Bring a torch to the sta-ble run!
Un flam-beau, cou-rons au ber-ceau!

It is Je-sus, good folk of the vil-lage;
C'est Je-sus, bon-nes gens du ha-meau,

Christ is born, and Mar-y's call-ing: Ah!
Le Christ est né, et Ma-rie ap-pel-le, Ah!

The Friendly Beasts

English

3. "I," said the cow, all white and red,
   "I have Him my manger for his bed.
   I gave Him hay to pillow his head."
   "I," said the cow, all white and red.

4. "I," said the sheep, with curly horn,
   "I gave Him my wool for his blanket warm;
   He wore my coat on Christmas morn."
   "I," said the sheep, with curly horn.

5. "I," said the dove, from rafters high,
   "Cooed Him to sleep that He should not cry;
   We cooed Him to sleep, my mate and I."
   "I," said the dove, from rafters high.

6. Thus every beast by some good spell
   In the stable dark was glad to tell
   Of the gift he gave Emmanuel,
   The gift he gave Emmanuel.

The Oxen

CHRISTMAS EVE, and twelve of the clock.
"Now they are all on their knees,"
An elder said as we sat in a flock
By the embers in hearthside ease.

We pictured the meek mild creatures where
They dwelt in their strawy pen,
Nor did it occur to one of us there
To doubt they were kneeling then.

So fair a fancy few would weave
In these years! Yet, I feel,
If someone said on Christmas Eve,
"Come; see the oxen kneel

"In the lonely barton by yonder coomb
Our childhood used to know,"
I should go with him in the gloom,
Hoping it might be so.

THOMAS HARDY

Neighbors of the Christmas Child

DEEP IN THE SHELTER of the cave,
  The ass with drooping head
Stood weary in the shadow, where
His master's hand had led.
About the manger oxen lay,
Bending a wide-eyed gaze
Upon the little newborn Babe,
Half worship, half amaze.
High in the roof the doves were set,
And cooed there, soft and mild,
Yet not so sweet as, in the hay,
The Mother to her Child.
The gentle cows breathed fragrant breath
To keep Babe Jesus warm,
While loud and clear, o'er hill and dale,
The cocks crowed, "Christ is born!"
Out in the fields, beneath the stars,
The young lambs sleeping lay,
And dreamed that in the manger slept
Another, white as they.

These were Thy neighbors, Christmas Child;
To Thee their love was given,
For in Thy baby face there shone
The wonder-light of heaven.

NORA ARCHIBALD SMITH

The Field Mice Go Caroling

A<small>T LAST</small> the Rat succeeded in decoying him to the table, and had just got seriously to work with the sardine-opener when sounds were heard from the fore-court without—sounds like the scuffling of small feet in the gravel and a confused murmur of tiny voices while broken sentences reached them—"Now, all in a line—hold the lantern up a bit, Tommy—clear your throats first—no coughing after I say one, two, three.—Where's young Bill?—Here, come on, do, we're all a-waiting—"

"What's up?" inquired the Rat, pausing in his labors.

"I think it must be the field-mice," replied the Mole, with a touch of pride in his manner. "They go round carol-singing regularly at this time of the year. They're quite an institution in these parts. And they never pass me over—they come to Mole End last of all; and I used to give them hot drinks, and supper too sometimes, when I could afford it. It will be like old times to hear them again."

"Let's have a look at them!" cried the Rat, jumping up and running to the door.

It was a pretty sight, and a seasonable one, that met their eyes when they flung the door open. In the fore-court, lit by the dim rays of a horn lantern, some eight or ten little field-mice stood in a semi-circle, red worsted comforters round their throats, their fore-paws thrust deep into their pockets, their feet jigging for warmth. With bright beady eyes they glanced shyly at each other, sniggering a little, sniffing and applying coat-sleeves a good deal.

As the door opened, one of the older ones that carried the lantern was just saying, "Now then, one, two, three!" and forthwith their shrill little voices uprose on the air, singing one of the old-time carols that their forefathers composed in fields that were fallow and held by frost, or when snow-bound in chimney corners, and handed down to be sung in the miry street to lamp-lit windows at Yule-time.

FROM *T<small>HE</small> W<small>IND IN THE</small> W<small>ILLOWS</small>* <small>BY</small> K<small>ENNETH</small> G<small>RAHAME</small>

We Three Kings of Orient Are

J.H. Hopkins, Jr.

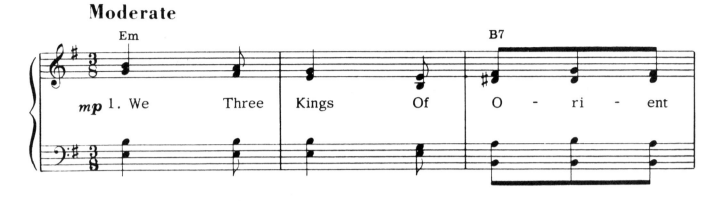

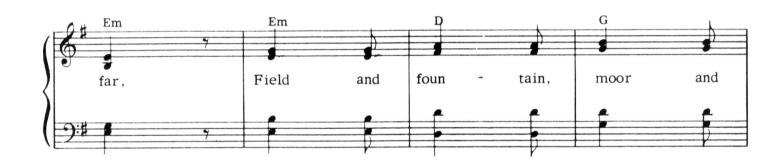

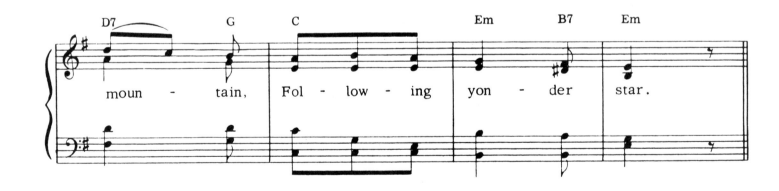

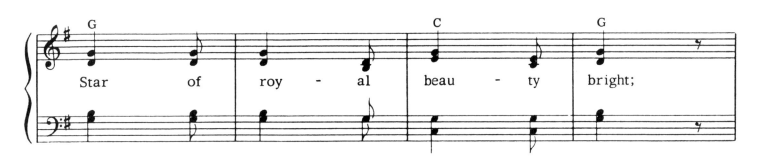

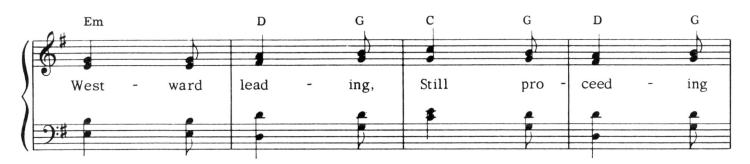

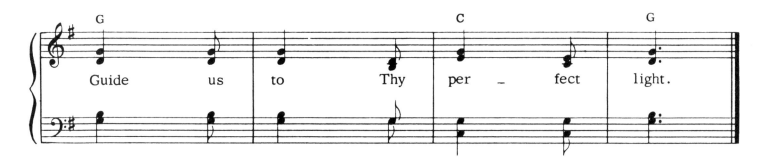

2. Born a King on Bethlehem plain,
   Gold I bring to crown Him again,
   King forever, ceasing never
   Over us all to reign.
       Refrain

3. Frankincense to offer have I,
   Incense owns a deity nigh:
   Prayer and praising, all men raising,
   Worship Him, God on high.
       Refrain

4. Myrrh is mine; its bitter perfume
   Breathes a life of gathering gloom;
   Sorrowing, sighing, bleeding, dying,
   Sealed in a stone cold tomb.
       Refrain

5. Glorious now behold Him arise,
   King and God, and sacrifice.
   Heaven sings Alleluia:
   Alleluia the earth replies.
       Refrain

As With Gladness Men of Old

Words by William Dix
Music by Conrad Kocher

1. As with gladness men of old Did the guiding star behold; As with joy they hail'd its light, Leading onward, beaming bright. So most gracious Lord, may we Evermore be led by thee.

2. As with joyful steps they sped To that lowly manger bed, There to bend the knee before Him who heav'n and earth adore, So may we with willing feet Ever seek Thy mercy seat.

3. As they offered gifts most rare
   At that manger rude and bare,
   So may we with holy joy,
   Pure and free from sin's alloy,
   All our costliest treasures bring,
   Christ, to Thee, our heav'nly King.

4. Holy Jesus, every day
   Keep us in the narrow way;
   And, when earthly things are past,
   Bring our ransomed souls at last
   Where they need no star to guide,
   Where no clouds Thy glory hide.

What Child Is This?

English

Moderato

mf 1. What Child is this,— Who, laid to rest— On Mary's lap,— is sleep-ing? Whom an-gels greet— with an-thems sweet, While shep-herds watch are keep-ing? This, this— is Christ the King,— Whom shep-herds guard— and an-gels sing: Haste, haste— to bring Him laud,— The Babe,— the Son— of Ma-ry!

2. Why lies He in such mean estate,
   Where ox and ass are feeding?
   Good Christian, fear, for sinners here,
   The silent word is pleading:
   Nails, spear, shall pierce Him through,
   The cross be born, for me, for you:
   Hail, hail, the Word made flesh,
   The Babe, the Son of Mary!

3. So bring Him incense, gold and myrrh,
   Come peasant, king to own Him,
   The King of kings salvation brings,
   Let loving hearts enthrone Him.
   Raise, raise the song on high,
   The Virgin sings her lullaby:
   Joy, joy, for Christ is born,
   The Babe, the Son of Mary!

Epiphany Cake

Baking and decorating a traditional Epiphany cake is a fun way to celebrate Old Christmas on January 6th, when the Wise Men arrived at the stable and beheld the Christ Child. Since Medieval times, it has been the custom to bake this holiday dessert, sometimes called a King's Cake, with a coin, charm, or nut hidden inside. The person who finds the prize is then dubbed "king" or "queen" of the feast. Sometimes two coins are hidden and two lucky diners are given this honor. The golden Epiphany cake that follows is baked in a tiara pan and decorated with candies to resemble a beautiful jeweled crown.

2 large silver coins
½ cup sugar
½ cup honey
½ cup (1 stick) margarine
1 cup cultured sour cream
2 eggs, well beaten
1 teaspoon lemon extract
2 cups cake flour
1½ teaspoons baking powder
½ teaspoon baking soda
½ pound candy fruit slices
¼ pound fruit-flavored gumdrops

Icing:
½ cup milk
2 tablespoons flour
½ cup (1 stick) butter
½ cup confectioners' sugar
¼ teaspoon yellow food coloring

1. Sterilize the 2 silver coins by dropping them in a small pan of boiling water. Drain.

2. Preheat the oven to 350°F.

3. Cream the sugar, honey, and margarine. Continue beating as you add the sour cream, eggs, and lemon extract.

4. Sift together the cake flour, baking powder, and baking soda. Gradually fold the flour mixture into the creamed mixture until absorbed. Do not beat. Pour the batter into a greased tiara pan and drop the silver coins into the batter in different locations. Bake for 30 minutes, or until a toothpick inserted in the center comes out clean.

5. To prepare the frosting: Combine the milk and flour in a saucepan and cook over medium heat for a bout 5 minutes, stirring constantly, until the mixture is very thick. Cool. Cream the butter and sugar. Add the milk paste and food coloring and whip until very fluffy.

6. Frost the cake and decorate the top with the candy fruit slices and gumdrops.

Note: Be sure to use large silver coins in this cake so that youngsters are not able to swallow their prize accidentally. Although a quarter is probably large enough, we recommend that you take the time to get half-dollars for use in this recipe. In any case, be sure that children understand that there are coins in the cake, and supervise them when they eat it (the coins will be found just beneath the top surface of the cake). Although the coins will be sterilized in the baking process, we recommend that you dip them in boiling water before you begin to work with the other ingredients, as is described in the first step of this recipe.

Serves 6 to 8.

The Three Kings

THREE KINGS came riding from far away,
    Melchior and Gaspar and Baltasar;
Three Wise Men out of the East were they,
And they travelled by night and they slept by day,
    For their guide was a beautiful, wonderful star.

The star was so beautiful, large and clear,
    That all the other stars of the sky
Became a white mist in the atmosphere;
And by this they knew that the coming was near
    Of the Prince foretold in the prophecy.

Three caskets they bore on their saddle-bows,
    Three caskets of gold with golden keys;
Their robes were of crimson silk, with rows
Of bells and pomegranates and furbelows,
    Their turbans like blossoming almond-trees.

And so the Three Kings rode into the West,
    Through the dusk of night over hills and dells,
And sometimes they nodded with beard on breast,
And sometimes talked, as they paused to rest,
    With the people they met at the wayside wells.

"Of the child that is born," said Baltasar,
    "Good people, I pray you, tell us the news;
For we in the East have seen his star,
And have ridden fast, and have ridden far,
    To find and worship the King of the Jews."

And the people answered, "You ask in vain;
    We know of no king but Herod the Great!"
They thought the Wise Men were men insane,
As they spurred their horses across the plain
    Like riders in haste who cannot wait.

And when they came to Jerusalem,
    Herod the Great, who had heard this thing,
Sent for the Wise Men and questioned them;
And said, "Go down unto Bethlehem,
    And bring me tidings of this new king."

So they rode away, and the star stood still,
  The only one in the gray of morn;
Yes, it stopped, it stood still of its own free will,
Right over Bethlehem on the hill,
  The city of David where Christ was born.

And the Three Kings rode through the gate and the guard,
  Through the silent street, till their horses turned
And neighed as they entered the great inn-yard;
But the windows were closed, and the doors were barred,
  And only a light in the stable burned.

And cradled there in the scented hay,
  In the air made sweet by the breath of kine,
The little child in the manger lay,
The Child that would be King one day
  Of a kingdom not human, but divine.

His mother, Mary of Nazareth,
  Sat watching beside his place of rest,
Watching the even flow of his breath,
For the joy of life and the terror of death
  Were mingled together in her breast.

They laid their offerings at his feet:
  The gold was their tribute to a King;
The frankincense, with its odor sweet,
Was for the Priest, the Paraclete;
  The myrrh for the body's burying.

And the mother wondered and bowed her head,
  And sat as still as a statue of stone;
Her heart was troubled yet comforted,
Remembering what the angel had said
  Of an endless reign and of David's throne.

Then the Kings rode out of the city gate,
  With a clatter of hoofs in proud array;
But they went not back to Herod the Great,
For they knew his malice and feared his hate,
  And returned to their homes by another way.

HENRY WADSWORTH LONGFELLOW

See Amid the Winter's Snow

English

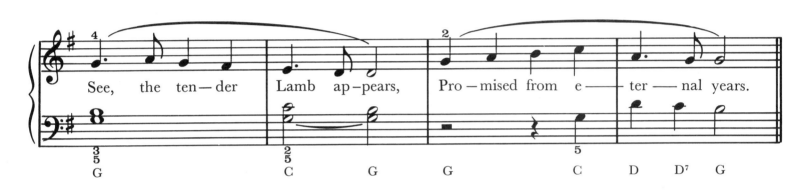

CHORUS

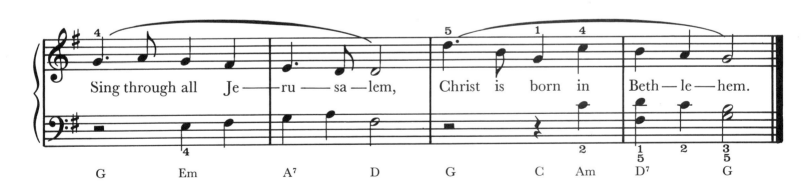

2. Lo, within a manger lies
He who built the starry skies;
He, who throned in height sublime,
Sits amid the Cherubim.
Chorus

3. Say, ye holy shepherds, say
What your joyful news today;
Wherefore have ye left your sheep
On the lonely mountain steep?
Chorus

4. "As we watched at dead of night,
Lo, we saw a wondrous light;
Angels singing peace on earth
Told us of the Savior's birth."
Chorus

5. Sacred Infant, all divine,
What a tender love was thine;
Thus to come from highest bliss
Down to such a world as this.
Chorus

6. Teach, O teach us, Holy Child,
By thy face so meek and mild,
Teach us to resemble Thee
In thy sweet humility.
Chorus

Good King Wenceslas

Words by John M. Neale

Moderately lively

1. Good King Wen - ces - las looked out On the Feast of Ste - phen,
When the snow lay round a - bout, Deep and crisp and e - ven.
Bright - ly shone the moon that night, Though the frost was cru - el,
When a poor man came in sight, Gath-'ring win - ter fu - el.

2. "Hither, page, and stand by me,
   If thou know'st it telling:
   Yonder peasant, who is he?
   Where and what his dwelling?"
   "Sire, he lives a good league hence,
   Underneath the mountain;
   Right against the forest fence,
   By Saint Agnes' fountain."

3. "Bring me flesh, and bring me wine,
   Bring me pinelogs hither;
   Thou and I shall see him dine
   When we bear them thither."
   Page and monarch forth they went,
   Forth they went together;
   Through the rude wind's wild lament
   And the bitter weather.

4. "Sire, the night is darker now,
   And the wind blows stronger;
   Fails my heart, I know not how,
   I can go no longer."
   "Mark my footsteps good, my page;
   Tread thou in them boldly.
   Thou shalt find the winter's rage
   Freeze thy blood less coldly."

5. In his master's steps he trod,
   Where the snow lay dinted;
   Heat was in the very sod
   Which the saint had printed.
   Therefore, Christian men be sure,
   Wealth or rank possesing,
   Ye who now will bless the poor,
   Shall youselves find blessing.

In the Bleak Mid-Winter

IN THE BLEAK mid-winter,
Frosty wind made moan,
Earth stood hard as iron,
Water like a stone;
Snow had fallen, snow on snow,
Snow on snow,
In the bleak mid-winter,
Long ago.

Our God, heaven cannot hold Him,
Nor earth sustain;
Heaven and earth shall flee away
When He comes to reign:
In the bleak mid-winter
A stable-place sufficed
The Lord God Almighty,
Jesus Christ.

Enough for Him, whom cherubim
Worship night and day,
A breastful of milk
And a mangerful of hay;
Enough for Him, whom angels
Fall down before,
The ox and ass and camel
Which adore.

Angels and archangels
May have gathered there,
Cherubim and seraphim
Thronged the air;
But only His mother
In her maiden bliss
Worshipped the Beloved
With a kiss.

What can I give Him,
Poor as I am?
If I were a shepherd
I would bring a lamb,
If I were a Wise Man
I would do my part—
Yet what can I give Him,
Give my heart.

CHRISTINA ROSSETTI

Skating

And in the frosty season, when the sun
Was set, and, visible, for many a mile,
The cottage-windows through the twilight blazed,
I heeded not the summons. Happy time
It was indeed for all of us: for me
It was a time of rapture! Clear and loud
The village clock tolled six. I wheeled about,
Proud and exulting, like an untired horse
That cares not for its home.
                                  All shod with steel,
We hissed along the polished ice, in games
Confederate, imitative of the chase
And woodland pleasures—the resounding horn,
The pack loud bellowing, and the hunted hare.
So through the darkness and the cold we flew,
And not a voice was idle.
                                  With the din
Meanwhile the precipices rang aloud.
The leafless trees and every icy crag
Tinkled like iron; while the distant hills
Into the tumult sent an alien sound
Of melancholy, not unnoticed; while the stars
Eastward were sparkling clear, and in the west
The orange sky of evening died away.

Not seldom from the uproar I retired
Into a silent bay; or sportively
Glanced sideways, leaving the tumultuous throng,
To cut across the reflex of a star—
Image, that, flying still before me, gleamed
Upon the glassy plain. And oftentimes,
When we had given our bodies to the wind,
And all the shadowy banks on either side
Came sweeping through the darkness, spinning still
The rapid line of motion, then at once
Have I, reclining back upon my heels,
Stopped short; yet still the solitary cliffs
Wheeled by me, even as if the earth had rolled
With visible motion her diurnal round.
Behind me did they stretch in solemn train,
Feebler and feebler; and I stood and watched
Till all was tranquil as a summer sea.

FROM *The Prelude* BY William Wordsworth

Crystal Lace Ice Cream Bracelets

1 cup all-purpose flour
1 cup finely chopped walnuts
½ cup light corn syrup
½ cup margarine
⅔ cup sugar
4 to 5 pieces crystallized ginger
6 drops yellow food coloring (optional)
½ gallon vanilla ice cream

1. Preheat the oven to 375°F. Mix the flour and nuts. In a saucepan, heat the corn syrup, margarine, sugar, and ginger to boiling, stirring constantly. Remove from the heat. Stir the flour mixture gradually into the syrup. Add the food coloring, if desired, and mix well.

2. Pour the batter into a greased 13"×9"×2" baking pan. Bake 5 minutes. Cool 3 minutes, or until the dough can be cut and lifted. If it is too crisp, return to oven for a minute or two to soften. Cut into 6"×1½" rectangles and form into bracelets. Cool until crisp. Nest a scoop of ice cream in each bracelet and serve.

Serves 6 to 8.

Hot Cocoa

Three 1-ounce squares unsweetened chocolate
3 tablespoons sugar
1½ teaspoons cinnamon
6 cups milk
Salt
3 egg whites
¾ teaspoon almond extract
One 1-ounce square semisweet chocolate or white chocolate

1. Heat the unsweetened chocolate, sugar, cinnamon, and milk and a pinch of salt in the top of a double boiler, stirring constantly, until chocolate melts.

2. Beat the egg whites and the almond extract until peaks form. Add the chocolate mixture gradually to the egg whites, beating constantly until foamy. Pour into cups and shave semisweet chocolate over each cup before serving.

Serves 6.

The Twelve Days of Christmas

English

* Repeat this measure as often as necessary, so that these lines may be sung in reverse order, each time
  ending with "Six geese a-laying."

Pear-Walnut Salad

4 large pears
Juice of 1 lemon
7 stalks celery, thinly sliced
½ cup walnuts, coarsely chopped
½ cup mayonnaise
1½ teaspoons prepared mustard
6 to 8 large lettuce leaves

1. Core and dice 3 of the pears. Dip them in lemon juice to prevent discoloration. Add the celery slices and walnuts to the pears and toss together.

2. In a seperate bowl, mix the mayonnaise and mustard together. Add this dressing to the salad and toss well.

3. Serve on individual beds of lettuce. Slice the remaining pear and garnish the top of each salad with the few pear slices.

Serves 6 to 8.

Sweet Baked Pears

4 large pears
1 cup water
1 cup brown sugar
¼ cup raisins
3 tablespoons butter
1 teaspoon cinnamon
½ teaspoon ground cloves

1. Butter a 9″ square baking pan. Preheat the oven to 350°F.

2. Core and slice the pears about ½″ thick and place in the buttered baking pan.

3. In a saucepan, boil together the water, brown sugar, raisins, butter, cinnamon, and cloves for about 5 minutes, or until ingredients are dissolved and a syrup forms.

3. Pour the boiling syrup over the pear slices. Bake for 10 minutes or until the pears are tender. (Serve as a side dish with almost any type of roast.)

Serves 6 to 8.

The Gift of the Magi

ONE DOLLAR and eighty-seven cents. That was all. And sixty cents of it was in pennies. Pennies saved one and two at a time by bulldozing the grocer and the vegetable man and the butcher until one's cheeks burned with the silent imputation of parsimony that such close dealing implied. Three times Della counted it. One dollar and eighty-seven cents. And the next day would be Christmas.

There was clearly nothing to do but flop down on the shabby little couch and howl. So Della did it. Which instigates the moral reflection that life is made up of sobs, sniffles, and smiles, with sniffles predominating.

While the mistress of the home is gradually subsiding from the first stage to the second, take a look at the home. A furnished flat at eight dollars per week. It did not exactly beggar description, but it certainly had that word on the lookout for the mendicancy squad.

In the vestibule below was a letter box into which no letter would go, and an electric button from which no mortal finger could coax a ring. Also appertaining thereunto was a card bearing the name "Mr. James Dillingham Young."

The "Dillingham" had been flung to the breeze during a former period of prosperity when its possessor was being paid thirty dollars per week. Now, when the income was shrunk to twenty dollars, the letters of "Dillingham" looked blurred, as though they were thinking seriously of contracting to a modest and unassuming D. But whenever Mr. James Dillingham Young came home and reached his flat above he was called "Jim" and greatly hugged by Mrs. James Dillingham Young, already introduced to you as Della. Which is all very good.

Della finished her cry and attended to her cheeks with the powder rag. She stood by the window and looked out dully at a gray cat walking a gray fence in a gray backyard. Tomorrow would be Christmas day, and she had only one dollar and eighty-seven cents with which to buy Jim a present. She had been saving every penny she could for months, with this result. Twenty dollars a week doesn't go far. Expenses had been greater than she had calculated. They always are. Only one dollar and eighty-seven cents to buy a present for Jim. Her Jim. Many a happy hour she had spent planning for something nice for him. Something fine and rare and sterling—something just a little bit near to being worthy of the honor of being owned by Jim.

There was a pier glass between the windows of the room. Perhaps you have seen a pier glass in an eight-dollar flat. A very thin and very agile person may, by observing his reflection in a rapid sequence of longitudinal strips, obtain a fairly accurate conception of his looks. Della, being slender, had mastered the art.

Suddenly she whirled from the window and stood before the glass. Her eyes were shining brilliantly, but her face had lost its color within twenty seconds. Rapidly she pulled down her hair and let it fall to its full length.

Now, there were two possessions of the James Dillingham Youngs in which they both took a mighty pride. One was Jim's gold watch that had been his father's and his grandfather's. The other was Della's hair. Had the Queen of Sheba lived in the flat across the air shaft, Della would have let her hair hang out the window some day to dry just to depreciate her majesty's jewels and gifts. Had King Solomon been the janitor, with all his treasures piled up in the basement, Jim would have pulled out his watch every time he passed, just to see him pluck at his beard from envy.

So now Della's beautiful hair fell about her, rippling and shining like cascade of brown waters. It reached below her knee and make itself almost a garment for her. And then she did it up again nervously and quickly. Once she faltered for a minute and stood still while a tear or two splashed on the worn red carpet.

On went her old brown jacket; on went her old brown hat. With a whirl of skirts and with the brilliant sparkle still in her eyes, she fluttered out the door and down the stairs to the street.

Where she stopped the sign read: "Mme. Sofronie. Hair Goods of All Kinds." One flight up Della ran, and collected herself, panting. Madame, large, too white, chilly, hardly looked the "Sofronie."

"Will you buy my hair?" asked Della.

"I buy hair," said Madame. "Take yer hat off and let's have a sight at the looks of it."

Down rippled the brown cascade.

"Twenty dollars," said Madame, lifting the mass with a practiced hand.

"Give it to me quick," said Della.

Oh, and the next two hours tripped by on rosy wings. Forget the hashed metaphor. She was ransacking the stores for Jim's present.

She found it at last. It surely had been made for Jim and no one else. There was no other like it in any of the stores, and she had turned all of them inside out. It was a platinum fob chain simple and chaste in design, properly proclaiming its value by substance alone and not by meretricious ornamentation—as all good things should do. It was even worthy of The Watch. As soon as she saw it she knew that it must be Jim's. It was like him. Quietness and value—the description applied to both. Twenty-one dollars they took from her for it, and she hurried home with the eighty-seven cents. With that chain on his watch Jim might be properly anxious about the time in any company. Grand as the watch was, he sometimes looked at it on the sly on account of the old leather strap that he used in place of a chain.

When Della reached home her intoxication gave way a little to prudence and reason. She got out her curling irons and lighted the gas and went to work repairing the ravages made by generosity added to love. Which is always a tremendous task, dear friends—a mammoth task.

Within forty minutes her head was covered with tiny, close-lying curls that made her look wonderfully like a truant schoolboy. She looked at her reflection in the mirror long, carefully, and critically.

"If Jim doesn't kill me," she said to herself, "before he takes a second look at me, he'll say I look like a Coney Island chorus girl. But what could I do—oh! what could I do with a dollar and eighty-seven cents?"

At seven o'clock the coffee was made and the frying pan was on the back of the stove and ready to cook the chops.

Jim was never late. Della doubled the fob chain in her hand and sat on the corner of the table near the door that he always entered. Then she heard his step on the stair away down on the first flight, and she turned white for just a moment. She had a habit of saying little silent prayers about the simplest everyday things, and now she whispered: "Please God, make him think I am still pretty."

The door opened and Jim stepped in and closed it. He looked thin and very serious. Poor fellow, he was only twenty-two—and to be burdened with a family! He needed a new overcoat and he was without gloves.

Jim stopped inside the door, as immovable as a setter at the scent of quail. His eyes were fixed upon Della, and there was an expression in them that she could not read, and it terrified her. It was not anger, nor surprise, nor disapproval, nor horror, nor any of the sentiments that she had been prepared for. He simply stared at her fixedly with that peculiar expression on his face.

Della wriggled off the table and went for him.

"Jim, darling," she cried, "don't look at me that way. I had my hair cut off and sold it because I couldn't have lived through Christmas without giving you a present. It'll grow out again—you won't mind, will you? I just had to do it. My hair grows awfully fast. Say 'Merry Christmas!' Jim, and let's be happy. You don't know what a nice—what a beautiful, nice gift I've got for you."

"You've cut off your hair?" asked Jim, laboriously, as if he had not arrived at that patent fact yet even after the hardest mental labor.

"Cut it off and sold it," said Della. "Don't you like me just as well, anyhow? I'm me without my hair, ain't I?"

Jim looked around the room curiously.

"You say your hair is gone?" he said, with an air almost of idiocy.

"You needn't look for it," said Della. "It's sold, I tell you—sold and gone, too. It's Christmas Eve, boy. Be good to me, for it went for you. Maybe the hairs of my head were numbered," she went on with a sudden serious sweetness, "but nobody could ever count my love for you. Shall I put the chops on, Jim?"

Out of his trance Jim seemed quickly to wake. He enfolded his Della. For ten seconds let us regard with discreet scrutiny some inconsequential object in the other direction. Eight dollars a week or a million a year—what is the difference? A mathematician or a wit would give you the wrong answer. The magi brought valuable gifts, but that was not among them. This dark assertion will be illuminated later on.

Jim drew a package from his overcoat pocket and threw it upon the table.

"Don't make any mistake, Dell," he said, "about me. I don't think there's anything in the way of a haircut or a shave or a shampoo that could make me like my girl any less. But if you'll unwrap that package you may see why you had me going a while at first."

White fingers and nimble tore at the string and paper. And then an ecstatic scream of joy; and then, alas! a quick feminine change to hysterical tears and wails, necessitating the immediate employment of all the comforting powers of the lord of the flat.

For there lay The Combs—the set of combs, side and back, that Della had worshiped for long in a Broadway window. Beautiful combs, pure tortoise shell, with jeweled rims—just the shade to wear in the beautiful vanished hair. They were expensive combs, she knew, and her heart had simply craved and yearned over them without the least hope of possession. And now, they were hers, but the tresses that should have adorned the coveted adornments were gone.

But she hugged them to her bosom, and at length she was able to look up with dim eyes and smile and say: "My hair grows so fast, Jim!"

And then Della leaped up like a little singed cat and cried, "Oh, oh!"

Jim had not yet seen his beautiful present. She held it out to him eagerly upon her open palm. The dull precious metal seemed to flash with a reflection of her bright and ardent spirit.

"Isn't it a dandy, Jim? I hunted all over town to find it. You'll have to look at the time a hundred times a day now. Give me you watch. I want to see how it looks on it."

Instead of obeying, Jim tumbled down on the couch and put his hands under the back of his head and smiled.

"Dell," said he, "let's put our Christmas presents away and keep 'em a while. They're too nice to use just at present. I sold the watch to get the money to buy your combs. And now suppose you put the chops on."

The magi, as you know, were wise men—wonderfully wise men who brought gifts to the Babe in the manger. They invented the art of giving Christmas presents. Being wise, their gifts were no doubt wise ones, possibly bearing the privilege of exchange in case of duplication. And here I have lamely related to you the uneventful chronicle of two foolish children in a flat who most unwisely sacrificed for each other the greatest treasures of their house. But, in a last word to the wise of these days, let it be said that of all who give gifts these two were the wisest. Of all who give and receive gifts, such as they are wisest. Everywhere they are wisest. They are the magi.

O. Henry

HOLIDAYS
THROUGHOUT THE YEAR

SONGS & STORIES

POEMS & RECIPES

Auld Lang Syne

Words by Robert Burns
Traditional Scottish Air

Should auld ac-quain-tance be for-got, And nev-er bro't to
here's a hand, my trust-y frien', And gie's a hand o'

mind? Should auld ac-quain-tance be for-got, And days of auld lang
thine; We'll tak' a cup o' kind-ness yet, For auld lang

Chorus

syne? For auld lang syne, my dear, For auld lang syne; We'll
syne.

tak' a cup o' kind-ness yet For auld lang syne. And syne.

1. **2.**

Hail! Hail! The Gang's All Here

Music by Arthur Sullivan

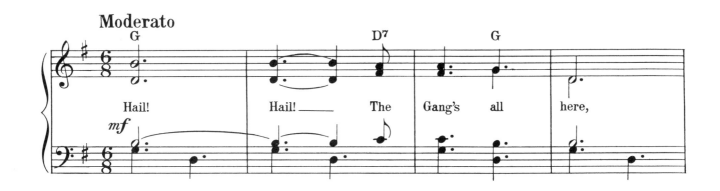

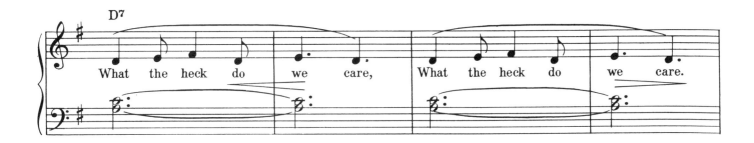

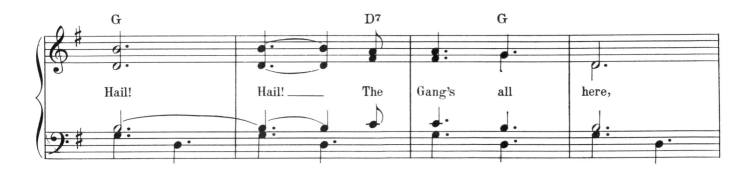

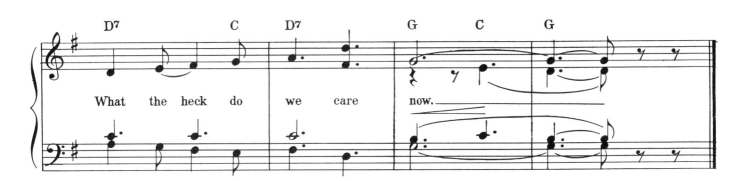

Ring Out, Wild Bells

Words by Alfred Tennyson
Music by Wolfgang Amadeus Mozart

Bright

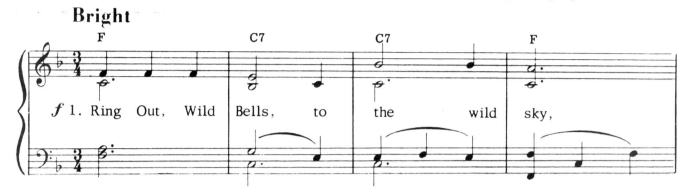

1. Ring Out, Wild Bells, to the wild sky,

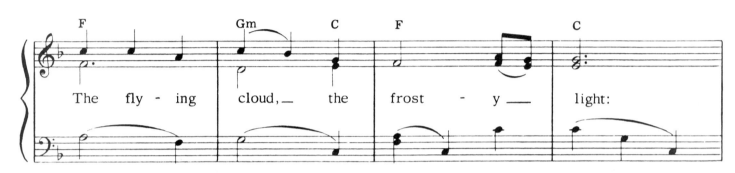

The fly - ing cloud, — the frost - y — light:

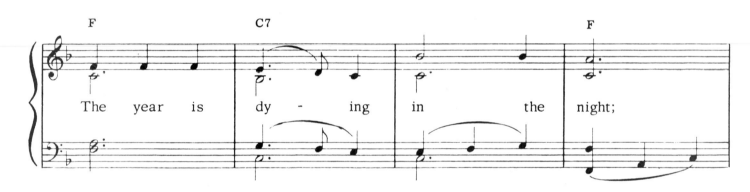

The year is dy - ing in the night;

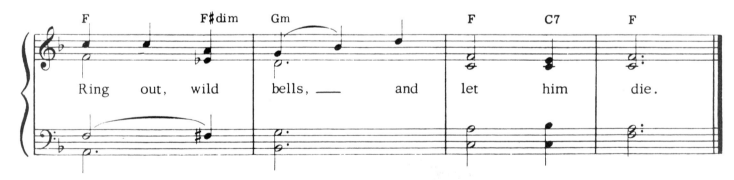

Ring out, wild bells, — and let him die.

2. Ring out the old, ring in the new,
   Ring, happy bells, across the snow:
   The year is going, let him go;
   Ring out the false, ring in the true.

3. Ring out false pride in place and blood,
   The civic slander and the spite;
   Ring in the love of truth and right,
   Ring in the common love of good.

Red Lentil Pottage

*Lentils are traditionally served at New Year to bring prosperity for the year to come.
In Italy, they say that each lentil you eat will bring one lucky day—so enjoy!*

2 cups beef broth
2 cups water
1 pound lentils
3 tablespoons olive oil
2 onions, minced
2½ pounds Italian sweet sausage
1 cup chopped celery (with leaves)
12 ounces canned tomato paste
1 teaspoon rosemary
2 bay leaves
Juice of 1 lemon
1 cup uncooked natural brown rice
Salt to taste
½ green pepper, finely chopped

1. Bring the broth and the 2 cups of water to a boil. Add the lentils and more
    water, if necessary, to cover. Bring back to a boil, remove from heat, and allow
    to soak for one hour.

2. In a large frying pan, heat the olive oil and sauté the onions until translucent.
    Add the sausage and brown. Drain off excess grease.

3. When the lentils have soaked an hour, add the sausage and onions to them.
    Then add the celery, tomato paste, rosemary, bay leaves, lemon juice, and
    brown rice. Add water to cover. Bring to a boil. Cover and simmer 2 hours.
    Check periodically to be sure the water has not been entirely absorbed by the
    rice. Add more water as needed.

4. Remove the sausage from the soup and cut into bit-size pieces, then return to
    the soup. Salt to taste and continue to simmer until flavors are well mixed.
    Sprinkle individual bowls of soup with chopped green pepper before serving.

Serves 6 to 8.

The Little Match Girl

IT WAS terribly cold; it snowed and was already almost dark, and evening come on, the last evening of the year. In the cold and gloom a poor little girl, bareheaded and barefoot, was walking through the streets. When she left her own house she certainly had slippers on, but of what use were they? They were very big slippers, and her mother had used them till then, so big were they. The little maid lost them as she slipped across the road, where two carriages were rattling by terribly fast. One slipper was not to be found again, and a boy had seized the other and run away with it. He thought he could use it very well as a cradle some day when he had children of his own. So now the little girl went with her little naked feet, which were quite red and blue with cold. In an old apron she carried a number of matches, and a bundle of them in her hand. No one had bought anything of her all day, and no one had given her a farthing.

Shivering with cold and hunger, she crept along, a picture of misery, poor little girl! The snowflakes covered her long fair hair, which fell in pretty curls over her neck; but she did not think of that now. In all the windows lights were shining, and there was a glorious smell of roast goose, for it was New Year's Eve. Yes, she thought of that!

In a corner formed by two houses, one of which projected beyond the other, she sat down cowering. She had drawn up her little feet, but she was still colder, and did not dare to go home, for she had sold no matches and did not bring a farthing of money. From her father she would certainly receive a beating; and, besides, it was cold at home, for they had nothing over them but a roof through which the wind whistled, though the largest rents had been stopped with straw and rags.

Her little hands were almost benumbed with the cold. Ah, a match might do her good, if she could only draw one from the bundle and rub it against the wall and warm her hands at it. She drew one out. R-r-atch! how it sputtered and burned! It was a warm, bright flame, like a little candle, when she held her hands over it; it was a wonderful little light! It really seemed to the little girl as if she sat before a great polished stove with bright brass feet and a brass cover. How the fire burned! How comfortable it was! But the little flame went out, the stove vanished, and she had only the remains of the burnt match in her hand.

A second was rubbed against the wall. It burned up, and when the light fell upon the wall it became transparent like a thin veil, and she could see through it into the room. On the table a snow-white cloth was spread; upon it stood a shining dinner service; the roast goose smoked gloriously, stuffed with apples and dried plums. And, what was still more splendid to behold, the goose hopped down from the dish and waddled along the floor, with a knife and fork in its breast, to the little girl. Then the match went out and only the thick, damp, cold wall was before her. She lighted another match. Then she was sitting under a beautiful Christmas tree; it was greater and more ornamented than the one she had seen through the glass door at the rich merchant's. Thousands of candles burned upon the green branches, and colored pictures like those in the print shops looked down upon them. The little girl stretched forth her hand toward them; then the match went out. The Christmas lights mounted higher. She saw them now as stars in the sky; one of them fell down forming a long line of fire.

"Now someone is dying," thought the little girl, for her old grandmother, the only person who had loved her, and who was now dead, had told her that when a star fell down a soul mounted up to God.

She rubbed another match against the wall; it became bright again, and in the brightness the old grandmother stood clear and shining, mild and lovely.

"Grandmother!" cried the child. "Oh, take me with you! I know you will go when the match is burned out. You will vanish like the warm fire, the warm food, and the great glorious Christmas tree!"

And she hastily rubbed the whole bundle of matches, for she wished to hold her grandmother fast. And the matches burned with such a glow that it became brighter than in the middle of the day; grandmother had never been so large or so in brightness and joy above the earth, very, very high, and up there was neither cold, nor hunger, now care—they were with God.

But in the corner, leaning against the wall, sat the poor girl with red cheeks and smiling mouth, frozen to death on the last evening of the old year. The New Year's sun rose upon a little corpse! The child sat there, stiff and cold, with the matches, of which one bundle was burned. "She wanted to warm herself," the people said. No one imagined what a beautiful thing she had seen and in what glory she had gone in with her grandmother to the New Year's Day.

HANS CHRISTIAN ANDERSEN

Keep Your Eyes on the Prize

African-American Spiritual

Paul and Si - las, bound in jail, Had no mon - ey for to make their bail,

Keep your eyes on the prize, Hold on, hold on.

Chorus

Hold on, hold on,

Keep your eyes on the prize, Hold on, hold on.

2. Paul and Silas began to shout,
   Jail door opened and they walked out,
   Keep your eyes on the prize,
   Hold on, hold on.
   Chorus

3. Freedom's name is mighty sweet,
   Soon one day we're gonna meet, *etc.*
   Chorus

4. Got my hand on the gospel plow,
   Wouldn't take nothing for my journey now,
   Chorus

5. The only chain that a man can stand,
   Is that chain of hand in hand,
   Chorus

6. The only thing that we did wrong,
   Stayed in the wilderness a day too long,
   Chorus

7. But the one thing that we did right,
   Was the day we started to fight,
   Chorus

8. We're gonna board that big Greyhound,
   Carryin' love from town to town.
   Chorus

9. We're gonna ride for civil rights,
   We're gonna ride for both black and white.
   Chorus

10. We've met jail and violence too,
    But God's love has seen us through,
    Chorus

11. Haven't been to heaven, but I've been told,
    Streets up there are paved with gold.
    Chorus

Oh Freedom

African-American Spiritual

2. No more fighting, no more fighting,
   No more fighting over me;
   Chorus

3. No more mourning, no more mourning,
   No more mourning over me;
   Chorus

4. No more weeping, no more weeping,
   No more mourning over me;
   Chorus

5. There'll be singing, there'll be singing,
   There'll be singing over me;
   Chorus

I Have a Dream

I HAVE A DREAM that my four little children will one day live in a nation where they will not be judged by the color of their skin, but by the content of their character.

I have a dream that one day, on the red hills of Georgia, the sons of former slaves and the sons of former slaveowners will be able to sit down together at the table of brotherhood.

❦ ❦ ❦

NONVIOLENCE is the answer to the crucial political and moral questions of our time; the need for man to overcome oppression and violence without resorting to oppression and violence.

Man must evolve for all human conflict a method which rejects revenge, aggression and retaliation. The foundation of such a method is love.

❦ ❦ ❦

I JUST WANT to do God's will. And He's allowed me to go to the mountain. And I've looked over, and I've seen the promised land. . . . So I'm happy tonight. I'm not worried about anything. I'm not fearing any man.

MARTIN LUTHER KING, JR.

Let Me Call You Sweetheart

Words and music by
Beth S. Whitson and Leo Friedman

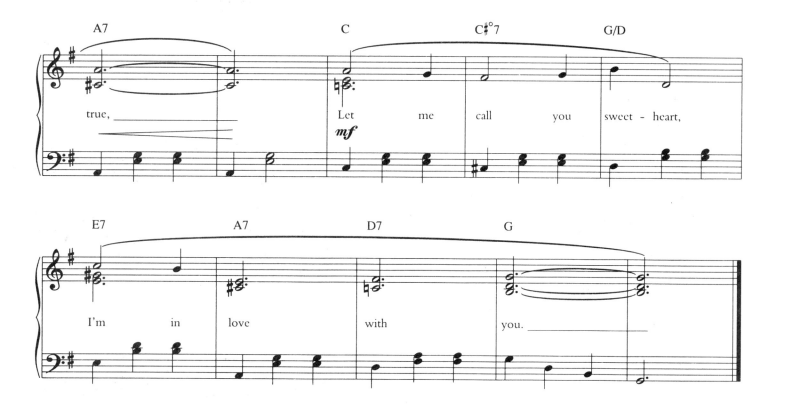

true, _____ Let me call you sweet - heart,

I'm in love with you. _____

I Love You Truly

Words and music by
Carrie Jacobs-Bond

Andante con amore

For I love you tru – ly, tru – ly, dear.
For you love me tru – ly, tru – ly, dear.

Valentine Cookies

½ cup shortening
¼ cup butter
1 cup sugar
2 eggs
½ teaspoon vanilla
½ teaspoon rose water (or orange flower water)
2½ cups all-purpose flour
1 teaspoon baking powder
½ teaspoon salt
⅓ teaspoon red food coloring
Red granulated sugar
Heart-shaped cookie cutter

1. Allow shortening and butter to soften, then cream these together with the sugar in a large mixing bowl. Beat in the eggs, vanilla, rose water, and red food coloring.

2. In a separate bowl, mix together the flour, baking powder, and salt.

3. Beat this dry mixture into the butter mixture until dough is well-blended.

4. Preheat oven to 400°F.

5. Roll dough ⅛-inch thick on a clean surface that has been dusted with flour. Cut into heart shapes, then sprinkle with red granulated sugar. Place on ungreased baking sheets and bake for 6 to 8 minutes, or until light golden brown.

6. Allow to cool on the baking sheets.

Makes 4 dozen cookies.

Sweetheart Cake

1 cup red grape juice
1 package unflavored gelatin
¾ cup margarine
1½ cups superfine sugar
1 teaspoon vanilla extract
2¼ cups cake flour
1 tablespoon baking powder
1 teaspoon salt
5 eggs
½ teaspoon red food coloring
1 cup cherry pie filling
1 maraschino cherry (or more, if desired)

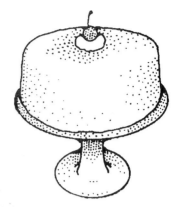

Pink Whipped Cream Topping:
½ pint heavy cream
1 teaspoon vanilla
1 tablespoon confectioners' sugar (or regular sugar)
Few drops red food coloring

1. Bring the grape juice to a boil in a saucepan. Add the gelatin and stir to dissolve. Reduce to a very low heat, add the margarine and sugar, and stir until dissolved. Remove from heat. Add the vanilla. Stir and allow to cool.

2. Sift together the cake flour, baking powder, and salt in large mixing bowl. (If you use self-rising cake flour, eliminate the baking powder and salt from the recipe.)

3. Separate the eggs while they are still cold. Allow the whites to stand at room temperature. Stir the yolks into the cooled syrup. Gradually add the syrup to the flour mixture, mixing until blended. Do not overbeat. When the egg whites are at room termperature, beat until soft peaks form. Pour them, all at once, over the batter and fold gently until completely blended. Add the food coloring and fold gently again.

4. Preheat the oven to 300°F. Grease and flour three 8″ cake pans. Pour the batter into the pans and bake for 30 minutes. A toothpick inserted into the center of the cake should come out clean when the cake is done.

5. Remove the pans and allow to stand for just a few minutes. Turn the cake layers out onto a rack to cool. Do not leave the cakes in the pans for more than a few minutes or they will be difficult to remove.

6. Spread half of the cherry pie filling over top of one cake layer, then top with another layer. Spread the remaining cherry pie filling over the second layer, then top with the third layer.

7. With an electric mixer, whip cream until it begins to thicken, while you gradually add the sugar, vanilla, and food coloring. Whip until thick but not stiff. Frost sides and top of cake with pink whipped cream. Top with maraschino cherry. Chill and serve.

Makes one 3-layer cake.

Hail to the Chief

Words by Sir Walter Scott
Music by James Sanderson

Majestically

Hail to the chief, who in tri - umph ad - vanc - es, Hon - ored and blessed be the ev - er - green_ pine!

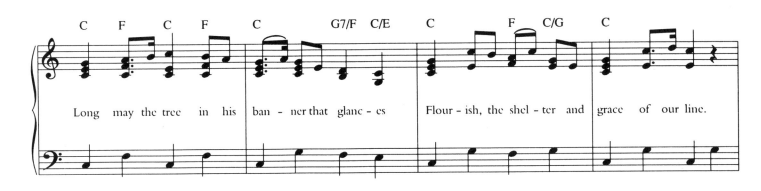

Long may the tree in his ban - ner that glanc - es Flour - ish, the shel - ter and grace of our line.

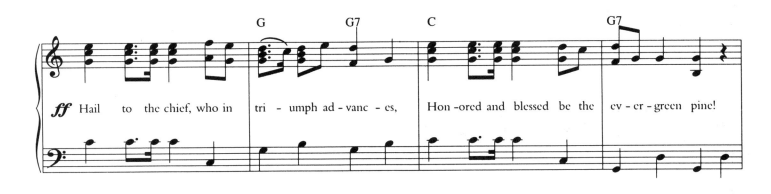

Hail to the chief, who in tri - umph ad - vanc - es, Hon - ored and blessed be the ev - er - green pine!

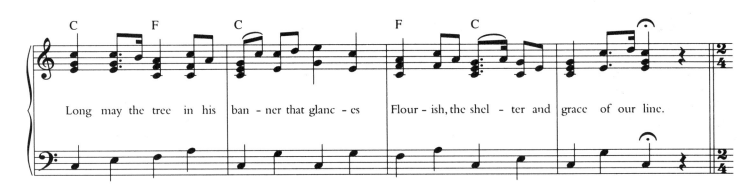

Long may the tree in his ban - ner that glanc - es Flour - ish, the shel - ter and grace of our line.

2. Ours is no sapling, chance-sown by the fountain,
   Blooming at Beltane, in winter to fade;
   When the whirlwind has stripp'd ev'ry leaf on the mountain,
   The more shall Clan-Alpine exult in her shade.
   Ours is no sapling, chance-sown by the fountain,
   Blooming at Beltane, in winter to fade;
   When the whirlwind has stripp'd ev'ry leaf on the mountain,
   The more shall Clan-Alpine exult in her shade.
   Moor'd in the rifted rock, proof to the tempest shock,
   Firmer he roots him, the ruder it blow;
   Menteith and Breadalbane, then, echo his priase again,
   "Roderigh Vich Alpine dhu, ho! ieroe!"

3. Row, vassals, row for the pride of the Highlands!
   Stretch to your oars for the evergreen pine!
   Oh, that the rosebud that graces yon islands,
   Were wreath'd in a garland around him to twine!
   Row, vassals, row, for the pride of the Highlands!
   Stretch to your oars for the evergreen pine!
   Oh, that the rosebud that graces yon islands,
   Were wreath'd in a garland around him to twine!
   O, that some seedling gem, worthy such noble stem,
   Honor'd and bless'd in their shadow might grow!
   Loud should Clan-Alpine then, ring from her deepmost glen,
   "Roderigh Vich Alpine dhu, ho! ieroe!"

George Washington

SOLDIER AND STATESMAN, rarest unison;
   High-poised example of great duties done
Simply as breathing, a world's honors worn
As life's indifferent gifts to all men born;
Dumb for himself, unless it were to God,
But for his barefoot soldiers eloquent,
Tramping the snow to coral where they trod,
Held by his awe in hollow-eyed content;
Modest, yet firm as Nature's self; unblamed
Save by the men his nobler temper shamed;
Never seduced through show of present good
By other than unsettling lights to steer
New-trimmed in Heaven, nor than his steadfast mood
More steadfast, far from rashness as from fear;
Rigid, but with himself first, grasping still
In swerveless poise the wave-beat helm of will;
Not honored then or now because he wooed
The popular voice, but that he still withstood;
Broad-minded, higher-souled, there is but one
Who was all this and ours, and all men's—Washington.

JAMES RUSSELL LOWELL

Abraham Lincoln

THIS MAN whose homely face you look upon,
   Was one of nature's masterful, great men;
Born with strong arms, that unfought battles won;
Direct of speech, and cunning with the pen.
Chosen for large designs, he had the art
Of winning with his humor, and he went
Straight to his mark, which was the human heart;
Wise, too, for what he could not break he bent.
Upon his back a more than Atlas-load,
The burden of the Commonwealth, was laid;
He stooped, and rose up to it, though the road
Shot suddenly downwards, not a whit dismayed.
Hold, warriors, councillors, kings! All now give place
To this dear benefactor of the race.

RICHARD HENRY STODDARD

Sugaring Off on Washington's Birthday

SUGAR MAPLES are traditionally tapped on Washington's Birthday—and sugaring off parties were held throughout February all over New England. The syrup is boiled until a soft ball is formed when dropped in cold water—then it is poured out in pans lined with snow and allowed to cool. The delicious maple syrup taffy which forms is then enjoyed by all the guests. Maple sugar is still a much-prized and special treat today. That's because so much of the sugar maple's sap actually boils away during the sugaring process, as described in this quaint excerpt from a 19th century cookbook.

Use a cauldron deeper than it is wide and never fill it more than half full to allow room for boiling up. Prepare a thick bed of faggots for fast, hot kindling. Since few people have the new sugaring-off houses, pile some brush to break the wind. He who figures to get more than one gallon of syrup from less than 35 gallons of sap is not good at figuring nor at making maple syrup.

If you'd like to have your own "sugaring off" party at home, here's a delicious maple syrup dessert that is traditionally enjoyed during Presidents' Day Week in New England. Be sure to use real maple syrup, not the artificially flavored kind, to create this lip-smacking sundae. If maple syrup is not available at your grocer, try a gourmet food store or holiday gift foods catalog.

Maple Walnut Sundae

1 cup maple syrup
⅓ cup light cream
¼ teaspoon cinnamon
½ teaspoon vanilla
½ cup chopped walnuts
1 quart chocolate or vanilla ice cream

1. In a saucepan, combine the syrup, the cream, and the cinnamon and bring the mixture to a boil, stirring constantly.

2. Reduce heat and allow to simmer for 2 to 3 minutes, until a very soft ball is formed when a bit of the mixture is dropped in cold water.

3. Remove from heat, then stir in the vanilla and walnuts. Serve hot over scoops of chocolate or vanilla ice cream.

Serves 4.

Danny Boy
Londonderry Air

Words by Frederick Weatherly
Traditional Irish Air

With feeling

mp Oh Dan-ny boy, the pipes, the pipes are call - ing, From glen to

glen and down the moun -tain - side. The sum - mer's gone and all the flow'rs are

dy - ing, 'Tis you, 'tis you must go and I must bide. But come ye

back when sum-mer's in the mead - ow, Or when the val - ley's hushed and white with

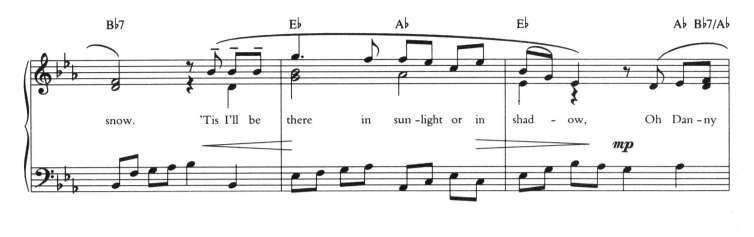

snow. 'Tis I'll be there in sun-light or in shad - ow, Oh Dan-ny

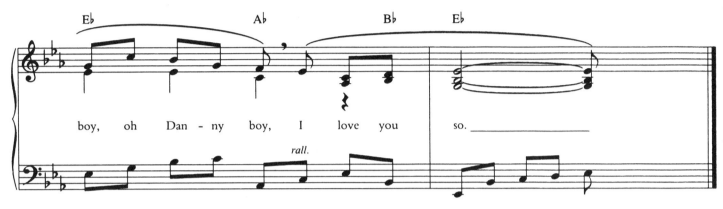

boy, oh Dan-ny boy, I love you so. _____

2. And if you come when all the flowers are dying,
And I am dead, as dead I well may be,
You'll come and find the place where I am lying,
And kneel and say and 'Ave' there for me.
And I shall hear, though soft you tread above me,
And all my dreams will warm and sweeter be.
If you only tell me that you love me,
Then I will sleep in peace until you come to me.

3. Oh Danny boy, the pipes, the pipes are calling,
From glen to glen and down the mountainside.
The summer's gone and all the flow'rs are dying,
'Tis you, 'tis you must go and I must bide.
But come ye back when summer's in the meadow,
Or when the valley's hushed and white with snow.
'Tis I'll be there in sunlight or in shadow,
Oh Danny boy, oh Danny boy, I love you so.

When Irish Eyes Are Smiling

Words by Chauncey Olcott and George Graff, Jr.
Music by Ernest R. Ball

Corned Beef and Cabbage

4- to 5-pound corned beef brisket
2 cloves garlic, minced
12 pearl onions
12 baby carrots (or 4 carrots, cut in rounds)
4 potatoes, quartered
1 green cabbage, wedged
1 teaspoon black pepper

1. Trim the brisket and place it in a large kettle. Cover with cold water.

2. Add garlic and bring to a boil. Reduce heat, cover, and simmer for 3 hours.

3. Skim and discard the fat which forms at the top of the liquid.

4. Add pearl onions, carrots, potatoes, and pepper. Cover and simmer 20 minutes.

5. Add cabbage and simmer 10 minutes more, or until all vegetables are tender. Drain and serve meat on a platter surrounded by vegetables. Carve the brisket in thin slices.

Cloverleaf Dinner Rolls

2 packages dry yeast
¼ cup warm water (105 to 115°F)
½ cup milk
½ cup (1 stick) margarine
½ cup sugar
½ teaspoon salt
1 egg, well beaten
4 to 5 cups bread flour

1. Mix the yeast with the warm water and allow to stand.

2. In a saucepan, heat the milk with the margarine, sugar, and salt until the margarine is melted and the mixture is well blended. Allow to cool for a few minutes. Add this to the yeast mixture. Add well-beaten egg and 2 cups of the flour to make a soft dough. Beat well. Add enough of the remaining flour, ½ cup at a time, until the dough is no longer sticky. Knead until smooth. Place dough in a greased bowl. Cover the bowl with plastic wrap, and set in a warm, draft-free place to rise for 1 hour. Roll out on a lightly floured surface.

3. To form cloverleaf rolls, roll small balls of the dough and place 3 of them in each muffin tin (the balls should be small enough so that the three balls will fit evenly). Cover and allow to rise again for 1 hour. Bake in a 425°F oven for 12 minutes.

Makes 12 rolls.

Hatikvoh
The Hope

Israeli Anthem

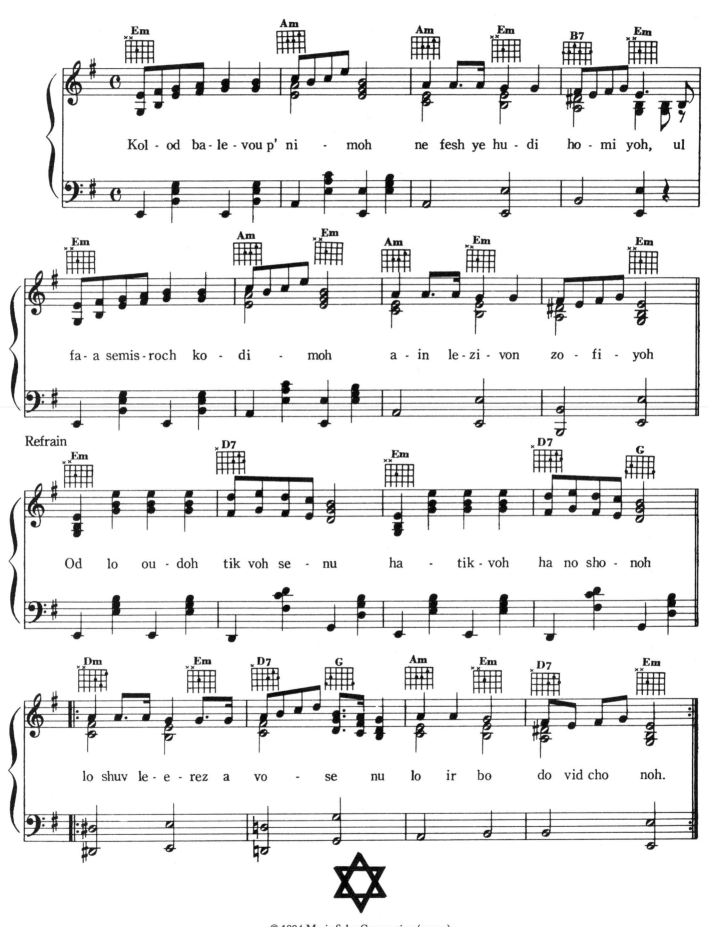

Kol - od ba - le - vou p' ni - moh ne fesh ye hu - di ho - mi yoh, ul

fa - a semis - roch ko - di - moh a - in le - zi - von zo - fi - yoh

Refrain

Od lo ou - doh tik voh se - nu ha - tik - voh ha no sho - noh

lo shuv le - e - rez a vo - se nu lo ir bo do vid cho noh.

Go Down, Moses

Solemnly

African-American Spiritual

When Israel was in E-gypt's land, Let my peo-ple go! Op-pressed so hard they could not stand, Let my peo-ple go!

Go down, Mos-es, way down in E-gypt's land,____ Tell ___ old Phar-aoh To let my peo-ple go!

2. The Lord told Moses what to do,
   Let my people go!
   To lead the Hebrew children through,
   Let my people go!
   Chorus

3. As Israel stood by the waterside, *etc.*
   At God's command it did divide, *etc.*
   Chorus

4. And when they reached the other shore,
   Then sang a song of triumph o'er.
   Chorus

5. Then Pharaoh said he'd go across,
   But Pharaoh and his host were lost.
   Chorus

6. Your foes shall not before you stand,
   And you'll possess fair Canaan's Land.
   Chorus

7. We need not always weep and mourn,
   And wear these slavery chains forlorn.
   Chorus

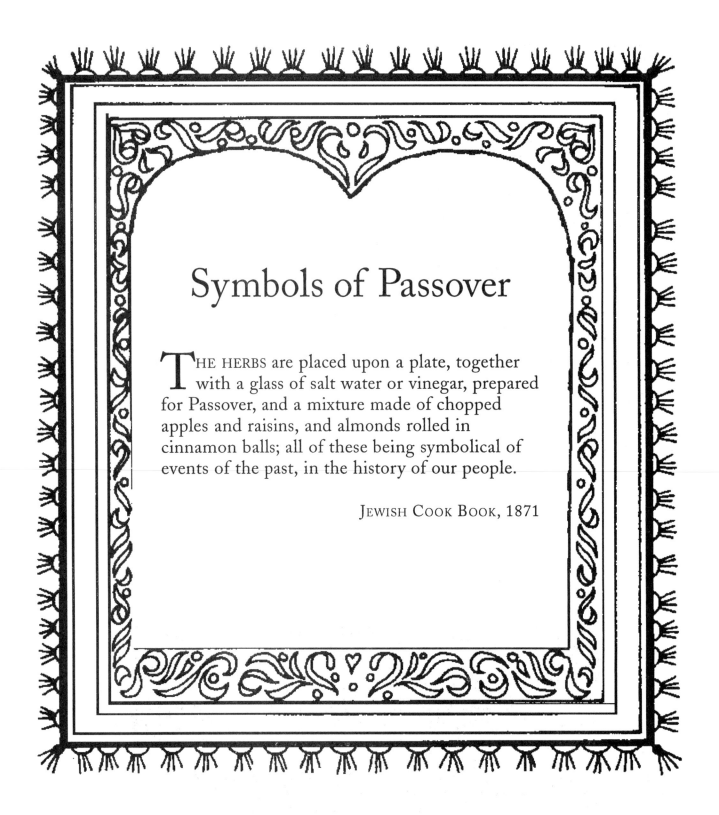

Symbols of Passover

THE HERBS are placed upon a plate, together with a glass of salt water or vinegar, prepared for Passover, and a mixture made of chopped apples and raisins, and almonds rolled in cinnamon balls; all of these being symbolical of events of the past, in the history of our people.

JEWISH COOK BOOK, 1871

Savory Beef Brisket

4- to 5-pound boneless beef brisket
1 teaspoon salt
1 medium onion, chopped
1 cup beef consommé
1 tablespoon Worcestershire sauce
½ teaspoon garlic powder
1 bay leaf, crumbled
½ teaspoon pepper

1. Trim and discard any fat from the brisket, then rub the brisket with salt.

2. Preheat the oven to 325°F.

3. Place a 30″×18″ sheet of heavy-duty aluminum foil in the bottom of a roasting pan (or large baking dish). Sprinkle the chopped onions on the foil to form a bed. Place the brisket on the bed of onions.

4. In a mixing bowl, stir together the consommé, Worcestershire sauce, garlic powder, bay leaf, and pepper. Pour the mixture over the brisket.

5. Wrap the foil over the top of the brisket and pinch to seal. Bake for three hours.

6. Remove the brisket to a platter. Top with cooked onions and serve.

Serves 8 to 10.

The Palms

Music by Jean Baptiste Faure
Words Traditional

1. O'er all the way green palms and blos-soms gay,
2. His word gave forth and peo-ples by its might,

Are strewn this day in fes-tal prep - a-ra-tion,
Once more re-gain freedom from deg - ra-da-tion,

Where Je-sus comes to wipe our tears a - way,___
Hu-man-i-ty to each doth give his right,___

E'en now the throng to wel-come him pre-pare;
While those in dark-ness find re-stored the light;

Join all and sing, His name de-clare,
Let ev-'ry voice re-sound with

ac - cla-ma - tion; Ho-san - na! praise ye the Lord!

Bless him who cometh to bring us Sal - va - tion! tion! tion!

Palms in Air

I know not where His islands lift
Their fronded palms in air,
I only know I cannot drift
Beyond His love and care.

JOHN GREENLEAF WHITTIER

Date Palm Cookies

1 cup butter
1 cup brown sugar
1 cup white sugar
3 eggs
4 cups flour
2 heaping teaspoons cream of tartar
1 rounded teaspoon baking soda
1 teaspoon vanilla extract

Date Filling:
2 cups chopped dates
1 cup sugar
1 cup cold water
1 tablespoon flour

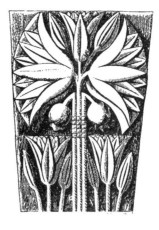

1. Cream the butter with the brown sugar and the white sugar. Add the eggs one at a time, mixing well.

2. Mix the flour with the cream of tartar and baking soda and gradually add to sugar mixture. Add vanilla and mix well.

3. Turn the dough out on a floured board. Add a bit more flour if the dough is too sticky to handle. Roll into a ball and cover the bowl with plastic wrap. Refrigerate for 30 minutes.

4. Roll out dough to a thickness of ¼″. Using a biscuit cutter, cut cookies and place on a greased baking sheet at least 2″ apart.

5. Preheat the oven to 350°F.

6. To make the filling: Cut the dates into small pieces with a wet pair of scissors. Combine all the ingredients and cook to boiling. Allow to cool.

7. Put a large spoonful of filling in the center of one cookie and top with another cookie, crimping the edges to make a tight seal. Bake for 10 to 12 minutes or until brown.

Makes 16 large cookies.

Hearts of Palm Salad

28 ounces hearts of palm (two 14-ounce cans)
8 ounces bamboo shoots (one 8-ounce can)
½ cup mayonnaise
2 teaspoons sugar
1 teaspoon mace
½ head leaf lettuce
Parsley

1. Drain the hearts of palm and bamboo shoots. Cut the palm into bite-size slices.

2. Mix together the mayonnaise, sugar, and mace. Add the dressing to the palm and bamboo just before serving.

3. To serve, place on a bed of leaf lettuce and sprinkle with fresh parsley.

Serves 6 to 8.

Mister Rabbit

Traditional

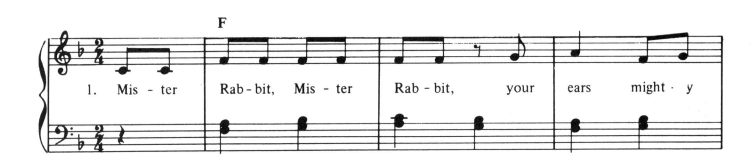

1. Mis - ter Rab - bit, Mis - ter Rab - bit, your ears might - y

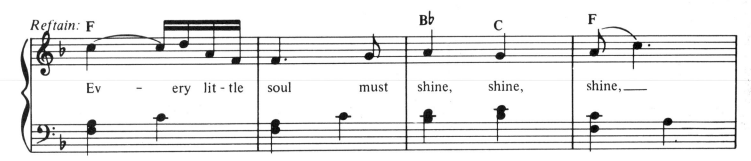

long. Yes, my Lawd, they-re put on wrong.___

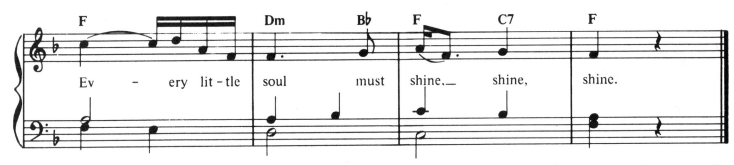

Refrain: Ev - ery lit - tle soul must shine, shine, shine,___

Ev - ery lit - tle soul must shine,___ shine, shine.

2. Mister Rabbit, Mister Rabbit, your coat mighty gray.
Yes, my Lawd, 'twas made that way.
Refrain

3. Mister Rabbit, Mister Rabbit, your feet mighty red,
Yes, my Lawd, I'm almost dead.
Refrain

4. Mister Rabbit, Mister Rabbit, your tail mighty white.
Yes, my lawd, and I'm getting out of sight.
Refrain

5. Mister Rabbit, Mister Rabbit, you look might thin.
Yes, my Lawd, been cutting through the wind.
Refrain

There Is a Green Hill

Traditional

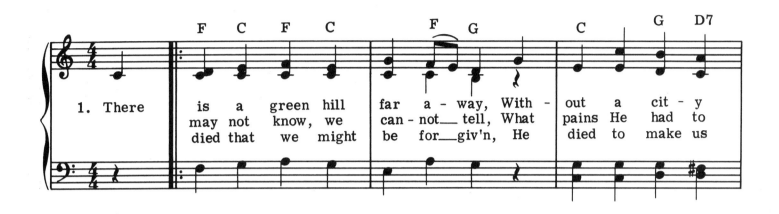

1. There is a green hill far a - way, With - out a cit - y
may not know, we can - not tell, What pains He had to
died that we might be for - giv'n, He died to make us

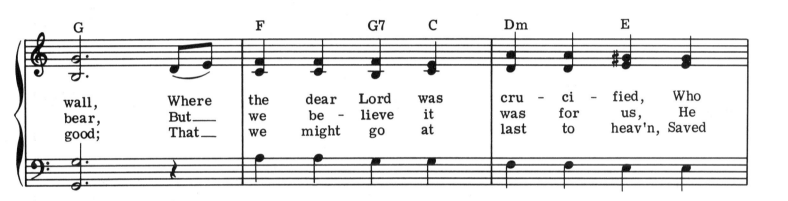

wall, Where the dear Lord was cru - ci - fied, Who
bear, But we be - lieve it was for us, He
good; That we might go at last to heav'n, Saved

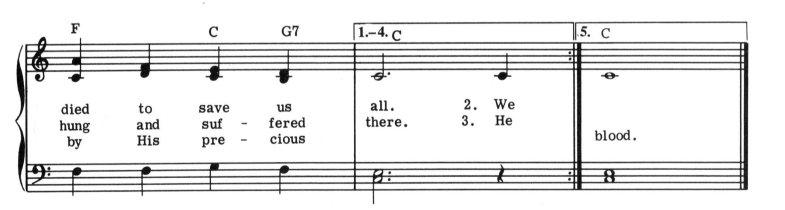

died to save us all. 2. We
hung and suf - fered there. 3. He
by His pre - cious blood.

4. There was no other good enough
   To pay the price of sin;
   He only could unlock the gate
   Of Heaven, and let us in.

5. O dearly, dearly has He loved,
   And we must love Him too,
   And trust in His redeeming blood;
   And try His words to do.

Voices of the Woods

Music by Anton Rubinstein
Words Anonymous

Calvary

Words by Henry Vaughan
Music by Paul Rodney

Andante espressivo

Rest, rest to the wear - y, Peace, peace to the soul;
O lay down thy bur - den, O come un - to me,

1. Though life may be drear - y, Earth is not thy goal! _

2. I _ will not for - sake thee, I _ will not for - sake thee, I will not for-

sake thee, Though all else should flee, though all else should flee. _

Were You There?

African-American Spiritual

1. Were you there when they cru-ci-fied my Lord? _____ Were you
2. Were you there when they laid him in the tomb? _____ Were you

there when they cru-ci-fied my Lord? Oh! _____ Some-times it
there when they laid him in the tomb?

caus-es me to trem-ble, broth-ers, trem-ble. Were you there when they cru-ci-fied my Lord?

April

APRIL COLD with dropping rain
Willows and lilacs brings again,
The whistle of returning birds,
And trumpet-lowing of the herds;
The scarlet maple-keys betray
What potent blood hath modest May;
What fiery force the earth renews,
The wealth of forms, the flush of hues;
What Joy in rosy waves outpoured,
Flows from the heart of Love, the Lord.

RALPH WALDO EMERSON

Hot Cross Buns

1 package dry yeast
1 cup lukewarm milk (105 to 115°F.)
¼ cup sugar
1 teaspoon salt
¼ cup soft margarine
2 eggs
1½ cups bread flour
2 to 2½ cups barley flour
2 tablespoons melted butter

Frosting:
½ stick melted margarine
¼ cup light cream
1 cup confectioners' sugar (approximately)
½ teaspoon almond extract

1. Stir the yeast into the milk and allow to stand.

2. In another bowl, beat together the sugar, salt, margarine, and eggs. Add yeast mixture to sugar mixture and blend. Beat in bread flour. Cover bowl with plastic wrap and allow dough to rise for 30 minutes in a warm, draft-free place.

3. Punch down the dough and gradually add barley flour to make a soft, pliable dough that is no longer sticky. Form into a ball and chill for ½ hour.

4. Roll out the dough on a board and cut into circles with a biscuit cutter or the rim of a glass. Place on a greased cookie sheet, brush with the melted butter or margarine, cover, and allow to rise for 1 hour. Bake in a preheated 400°F oven for about 12 minutes, or until golden brown.

5. While the buns are baking, prepare the frosting: Mix melted margarine and cream. Gradually beat in confectioners' sugar until frosting is thick and smooth (you may not need the whole cup called for). Add the almond extract and stir. Use a pastry bag to form a cross of frosting on the top of each bun.

Makes 20 buns.

Crown Roast of Lamb

1 crown roast of lamb
4 cups chicken stock
14 glazed onions

Ask the butcher to prepare a crown roast. Allow 2 chops per person. (A crown roast is a double piece of the loin, with 14 chops.)

1. Preheat the oven to 375°F. Set the roast in ½ cup of the chicken stock in a shallow roasting pan. Wrap each chop tip with a piece of aluminum foil and place the pan on a low shelf of the oven. Roast at 375°F for 10 minutes, then reduce heat to 350°F, pour 1 cup of stock over the roast, and continue basting frequently with the pan juices. As the juices evaporate, add additional stock every 15 to 20 minutes. A meat thermometer should read 170°F when the roast is done. The meat should be pink, not well done. Allow about 15 minutes a pound.

2. Skim off the fat and pour the pan juices through a sieve and boil. Pour into a sauceboat and serve with the roast.

3. Cap each rib with a glazed onion or a large pitted olive (or you can use chop frills). Fill the crown with wild rice.

Serves 6 to 8.

Meringue Easter Eggs

4 egg whites
⅛ teaspoon salt
¼ teaspoon cream of tartar
1 cup superfine sugar
½ teaspoon anise extract
6 drops yellow food coloring
6 drops blue food coloring

1. Preheat the oven to 225°F.

2. Beat the egg whites with the salt and cream of tartar to a soft foam. Sprinkle the sugar over the egg whites 1 tablespoon at a time, mixing until incorporated. Beat in the anise extract. Divide the egg mixture in half and add 6 drops yellow food coloring to one half and 6 drops blue food coloring to the other half. Beat until stiff.

3. Scoop by one tablespoon at a time onto a sheet of aluminum foil placed over a baking sheet. Bake 1 hour. Turn off oven and allow the meringues to dry completely in the oven.

4. Store in a covered tin. Do not refrigerate.

Makes 16 large meringues.

Little Things

Traditional

Lit - tle drops of wa - ter, Lit - tle grains of sand, Make the might - y
And the lit - tle mo - ments, Hum - ble though they be, Make the might - y

o - cean And the beau - teous land, And the beau - teous land.
a - ges Of e - ter - ni - ty, Of e - ter - ni - ty.

Fruitful Fields Are Waving

Traditional

Fruit - ful fields are wav - ing With the gold - en grain;

Peace - ful herds are graz - ing On the ver - dant plain.

Dona Nobis Pacem

Traditional

Do - na no - bis pa - cem, pa - cem,
Do - na__ no - bis pa - cem. Do -
na no - bis pa - cem, Do - na no - bis
pa - cem. Do - na no - bis__
pa - cem, Do - na no - bis pa - cem.

The World Beautiful

SWEET IS THE BREATH of Morn, her rising sweet
With charm of earliest birds; pleasant the Sun
When first on this delightful land he spreads
His orient beams, on herb, tree, fruit, and flower,
Glistening with dew; fragrant the fertile Earth
After soft showers; and sweet the coming on
Of grateful Evening mild; then silent Night
With this her solemn bird, and this fair Moon,
And these the gems of Heaven, her starry train.

FROM *PARADISE LOST* BY JOHN MILTON

Seven-Grain Dinner Loaf

1 package dry yeast
¼ cup warm water (105° to 115°F)
1½ cups hot water
⅓ cup brown sugar
1 teaspoon salt
3 tablespoons shortening
½ cup barley flour
½ cup buckwheat flour
½ cup soy flour
2½ cups bread flour
½ cup instant oatmeal
½ cup cooked brown rice
3 to 5 cups whole wheat flour
2 tablespoons melted butter

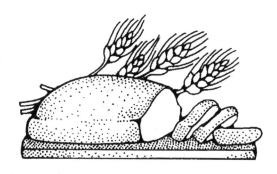

1. Stir the yeast into the ¼ cup warm water and let stand.

2. Stir together the 1½ cups hot water, brown sugar, salt, and shortening. (Hot water from the faucet is fine; if the water is too hot, it will kill the yeast.)

3. Add the yeast mixture to the sugar mixture, stirring until blended. To this mixture, add the barley, buckwheat, soy, and bread flours and then the oatmeal and cooked brown rice ½ cup at a time, mixing until they are incorporated well. Add the whole wheat flour a little at a time until dough is no longer sticky and can be handled. Form into a ball and place in a greased bowl. Cover bowl with plastic wrap, and let rise in a warm, draft-free place for 1½ to 2 hours, or until the dough doubles in size.

4. Remove dough from bowl and knead on a floured surface. Divide into halves and place each half onto a greased 9″×5″×2¾″ loaf pan. Cover with plastic wrap or a cloth and let rise for another 2 hours in a warm, draft-free place until doubled.

5. Bake in a preheated 375°F oven for 45 minutes. Brush with melted butter the last 15 minutes.

Makes 2 loaves.

Woodman, Spare That Tree!

Words by George Pope Morris
Music by Henry Russell

Andante con espressione

1. Wood - man, spare that tree! _____ Touch not a sin - gle
2. That old fa - mil - iar tree! _____ Whose glo - ry and re -

bough; In youth it shel - ter'd me, _____ And
nown; Are spread o'er land and sea, _____ And

I'll pro - tect it now. 'Twas my fore - fa - ther's
would'st thou hack it down? Wood - man, for - bear thy

hand _____ That plac'd it near his cot, There wood - man let _____ it
stroke! _____ Cut not its earth - bound ties, Oh, spare that a - ged

stand, _____ Thy axe shall harm it not!
oak, _____ Now tow - 'ring to the skies.

3. When but an idle boy,
   I sought its grateful shade;
   In all their gushing joy
   Here, too, my sisters played.
   My mother kissed me here;
   My father pressed my hand—
   Forgive this foolish tear,
   But let that old oak stand.

4. My heart-strings round thee cling,
   Close as thy bark, old friend!
   Here shall the wild-bird sing,
   And still thy branches bend.
   Old tree! the storm still brave!
   And, woodman, leave the spot;
   While I've a hand to save,
   Thy axe shall harm it not.

Hot Apple Pie à la Mode

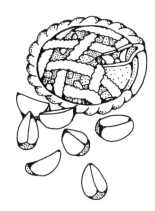

6 McIntosh apples
½ cup raisins
1 cup sugar
2 tablespoons cinnamon
Juice of 1 lemon
2 tablespons butter
1 quart French vanilla ice cream

Pastry:
½ teaspoon salt
2 cups flour
¾ cup shortening
½ cup cold water (or less)

1. Peel and core the apples and cut into slices. Add the raisins, sugar, cinnamon, and lemon juice. Mix well. Cover with plastic wrap and set aside (stirring occasionally) while you pepare the pastry. A thick syrup will form, and should coat the apples.

2. To make the pastry: Mix the salt with the flour and cut in the shortening until the mixture is the consistency of coarse cornmeal. Gradually add cold water until a dough forms. Divide the dough in half, roll each half into a ball, and chill for 30 minutes.

3. Preheat the oven to 350°F.

4. Roll out one ball of dough into a circle and place in a pie pan. Pour the filling into this crust (the pie should be quite full). Dot the top of the filling with butter. Roll out the other ball of dough, place it on top of the filling, and crimp around the edges with a fork. Cut steam slits in the top of the crust.

5. Place the pie pan on a cookie sheet to avoid oven spills. Bake 50 minutes.

6. Serve the pie hot. Scoop French vanilla ice cream onto each portion.

Serves 6 to 8.

The Planting of the Apple Tree

COME, LET US PLANT the apple tree.
Cleave the tough greensward with the spade;
Wide let its hollow bed be made;
There gently lay the roots, and there
Sift the dark mold with kindly care,
 And press it o'er them tenderly,
As, round the sleeping infant's feet
We softly fold the cradle sheet;
 So plant we the apple tree.

What plant we in this apple tree?
Buds, which the breath of summer days
Shall lengthen into leafy sprays;
Boughs where the thrush, with crimson breast,
Shall haunt and sing and hide her nest;
 We plant, upon the sunny lea,
A shadow for the noontide hour,
A shelter from the summer shower,
 When we plant the apple tree.

What plant we in this apple tree?
Sweets for a hundred flowery springs
To load the May wind's restless wings,
When, from the orchard row, he pours
Its fragrance through our open doors;
 A world of blossoms for the bee,
Flowers for the sick girl's silent room,
For the glad infant sprigs of bloom,
 We plant with the apple tree.

What plant we in this apple tree?
Fruits that shall swell in sunny June,
And redden in the August noon,
And drop, when gentle airs come by,
That fan the blue September sky,
 While children come, with cries of glee,
And seek them where the fragrant grass
Betrays their bed to those who pass,
 At the foot of the apple tree.

And when, above this apple tree,
The winter stars are quivering bright,
And winds go howling through the night,
Girls, whose young eyes o'erflow with mirth,
Shall peel its fruit by cottage hearth,
   And guest in prouder homes shall see,
Heaped with the grape of Cintra's vine
And golden orange of the line,
   The fruit of the apple tree.

The fruitage of this apple tree
Winds, and our flag of stripe and star,
Shall bear to coasts that lie afar,
Where men shall wonder at the view,
And ask in what fair groves they grew;
   And sojourners beyond the sea
Shall think of childhood's careless day
And long, long hours of summer play,
   In the shade of the apple tree.

Each year shall give this apple tree
A broader flush of roseate bloom,
A deeper maze of verdurous gloom,
And loosen, when the frost clouds lower,
The crisp brown leaves in thicker shower.
   The years shall come and pass, but we
Shall hear no longer, where we lie,
The summer's songs, the autumn's sigh,
   In the boughs of the apple tree.

And time shall waste this apple tree.
Oh, when its aged branches throw
Thin shadows on the ground below,
Shall fraud and force and iron will
Oppress the weak and helpless still?
   What shall the tasks of mercy be,
Amid the toils, the strifes, the tears,
Of those who live when length of years
   Is wasting this apple tree?

"Who planted this old apple tree?"
The children of that distant day
Thus to some aged man shall say;
And, gazing on its mossy stem,
The gray-haired man shall answer them:
   "A poet of the land was he,
Born in the rude but good old times;
'Tis said he made some quaint old rhymes
   On planting the apple tree."

WILLIAM CULLEN BRYANT

Now Is the Month of Maying

Words and music by
Thomas Morley

2. The spring, clad all in gladness,
Doth laugh at winter's sadness,
Fa la la la la la la la la, Fa la la la la la la.
And to the bagpipes sound,
The nymphs tread out their ground.
Fa la la la la, fa la la la la la la la la la la.

3. Fie, then! Why sit we musing,
Youth's sweet delight refusing?
Fa la la la la la la la la, Fa la la la la la la.
Say dainty nymphs, and speak,
Shall we play barley break?
Fa la la la la, fa la la la la la la la la la la.

While Strolling Through the Park One Day

Words and Music by
Ed Haley and Robert A. Keiser

Allegro moderato

While strol-ling thru the park one day, In the mer-ry month of May; I was tak-en by sur-prise, by a pair of ro-guish eyes, In a mo-ment, my poor heart she stole a-way. A smile was all she gave to me. Of course, we were as hap-py as could be Ah! I im-me-di-ate-ly rais'd my hat, And made a po-lite re-mark; I nev-er shall for-get, that love-ly af-ter-noon, I met her at the foun-tain in the park.

(Dance Step)

Song on May Morning

NOW THE BRIGHT morning star, Day's harbinger,
Comes dancing from the East, and leads with her
The flowery May, who from her green lap throws
The yellow cowslip and the pale primrose.
Hail, bounteous May, that doth inspire
Mirth, and youth, and warm desire;
Woods and groves are of thy dressing,
Hill and dale doth boast thy blessing.
Thus we salute thee with our early song,
And welcome thee, and wish thee long.

JOHN MILTON

Fair May

THEN CAME FAIR MAY, the fairest maid on ground,
  Deck'd all with dainties of her season's pride,
And throwing flowers out of her lap around:
Upon two brethren's shoulders she did ride;
The twins of Leda, which on either side
Supported her like to their sovereign queen.
Lord! how all creatures laughed when her they spied,
And leapt and danced as they had ravish'd been,
And Cupid's self about her fluttered all in green.

EDMUND SPENSER

Cielito Lindo
Beautiful Heaven

Words and music by
Quirino Mendoza y Cortéz

Ay! ay! ay! ay! ____ Love is but a dream, ____ He

plays with hearts, then rends them a - part, And leaves but grief and an-guish.

1. 2.

D.S. al Fine

Chiapanecas

Mexican Hat Dance

Broiled Mexican Chicken With Guacamole Relish

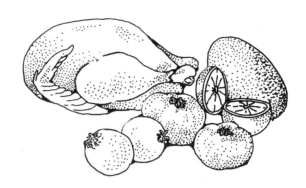

Garlic salt
6 chicken breasts, split in half
Juice of 2 lemons
1 cup vegetable oil
Flour tortillas

Guacamole Relish:
2 medium tomatoes, chopped
½ cup minced onion
2 jalapeño peppers, chopped
1 ripe avocado, chopped
Juice of 1 lemon

1. Sprinkle the garlic salt on the chicken breasts and marinate them in the juice of 2 lemons and oil for at least 1 hour.

2. Preheat the broiler or grill. If you use the broiler, oil the broiler pan and place it on the second position from the top in an electric oven or the middle or low position in a gas oven. The idea is not to broil too fast.

3. To prepare relish, mix the tomatoes, onions, jalapeños, and avocado. Sprinkle with lemon juice, then mash with a fork.

4. Spread the relish over the chicken breasts and serve with flour tortillas (or you can serve the guacamole relish on the side).

Serves 6.

Sopaipillas

3 cups unsifted all-purpose flour
½ teaspoon salt
1 tablespoon baking powder
3 tablespoons margarine
3 eggs
3 tablespoons sugar
⅓ cup water (or less)
Vegetable oil
⅓ cup sugar
½ teaspoon cinnamon

1. Sift the flour with the salt and baking powder. Cut the margarine into the flour mixture.

2. Beat the eggs with the 3 tablespoons sugar and add to the flour mixture. Add water to make a dough just firm enough to roll. Cover the bowl and let stand 1 hour.

3. Roll out the dough ¼-inch thick on a lightly floured board and cut into 3″ squares. Deep-fry in vegetable oil. When the sopaipillas are brown on one side, turn over to brown the other. While sopaipillas drain on paper towels, mix the cinnamon and the sugar together. Roll the sopaipillas in cinnamon-and-sugar mixture and serve immediately.

Makes 12.

A Boy's Best Friend Is His Mother

Words and music by
J.P. Skelly

While __ plod-ding on our way, the toil-some road of life, How

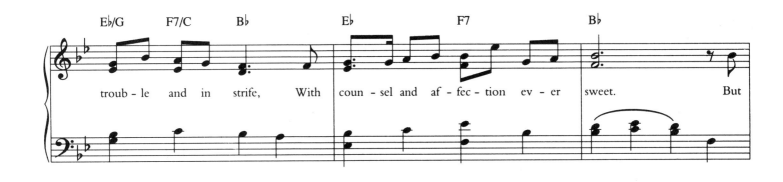

few the friends that dai-ly there we meet. Not __ man-y will stand by in

troub-le and in strife, With coun-sel and af-fec-tion ev-er sweet. But

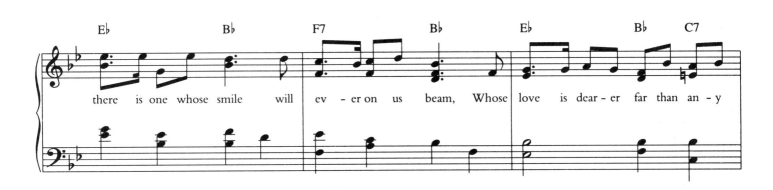

there is one whose smile will ev-er on us beam, Whose love is dear-er far than an-y

2. Though all the world may frown, and ev'ry friend depart,
   She never will forsake us in our need.
   Our refuge evermore, is still within her heart,
   For us her loving sympathy will plead.
   Her pure and gentle smile, forever cheers our way,
   'Tis sweeter and 'tis purer than all other.
   When she goes from earth away,
   We'll find out while we stray,
   A boy's best friend is his mother.
   Chorus

3. Her fond and gentle face, not long may greet us here,
   Then cheer her with our kindness and our love.
   Remember at her knee in childhood bright and dear,
   We heard her voice like angels from above.
   Though after years may bring their gladness or their woe,
   Her love is sweeter far than any other.
   And our longing heart will learn,
   Wherever we may turn,
   A boy's best friend is his mother.
   Chorus

Home, Sweet Home

Words by John Howard Payne
Music by Henry R. Bishop

seek _____ through the world, is ne'er met _____ with else - where.

Chorus

Home, home, _____ sweet, sweet home, There's no _____ place like

home, There's no place like home.

rall.

2. I gaze on the moon as I tread the drear wild,
   And feel that my mother now thinks of her child,
   As she looks on that moon from our own cottage door,
   Through the woodbine whose fragrance shall cheer me no more.
       Chorus

3. An exile from home, splendor dazzles in vain;
   Oh, give me a lowly thatched cottage again;
   The birds singing gaily, that came at my call,
   Give me them, and that peace of mind, dearer than all.
       Chorus

The Battle Hymn of the Republic

Words by Julia Ward Howe
Music Traditional

Majestically

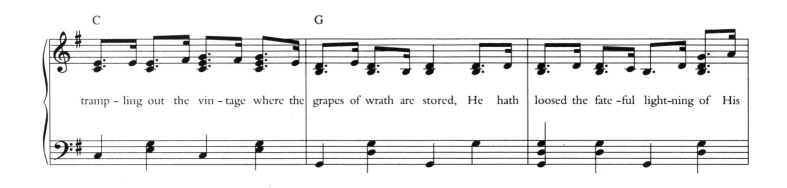

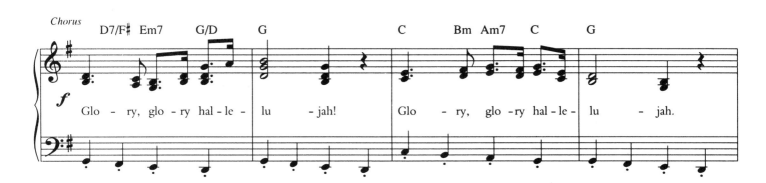

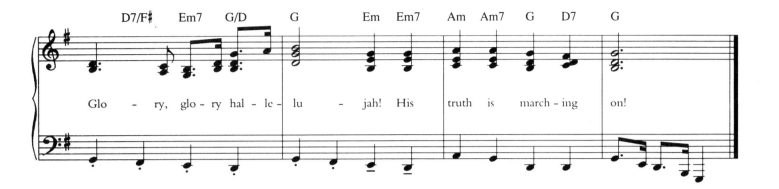

Glo - ry, glo - ry hal - le - lu - jah! His truth is march - ing on!

2. I have seen Him in the watchfires of a hundred circling camps,
   They have builded Him an altar in the evening dews and damps,
   I can read His righteous sentence by the dim and flaring lamps,
   His day is marching on.
      Chorus

3. I have read a fiery gospel writ in burnished rows of steel:
   "As ye deal with My contemners, so with you My grace shall deal."
   Let the Hero, born of woman, crush the serpent with His heel,
   Since God is marching on.
      Chorus

4. He has sounded forth the trumpet that shall never call retreat,
   He is sifting out the hearts of men before His judgment seat.
   Oh, be swift, my soul, to answer Him, be jubliant, my feet!
   Our God is marching on.
      Chorus

5. In the beauty of the lilies, Christ was born across the sea,
   With a glory in His bosom that transfigures you and me,
   As He died to make men holy, let us die to make men free,
   While God is marching on.
      Chorus

Amazing Grace

Words by John Newton
Traditional Scottish Air

Fervently

f A - maz - ing grace, how sweet the sound, That saved a wretch like me. I once was lost, but now I'm found, Was blind, but now I see.

2. 'Twas grace that taught my heart to fear,
And grace my fears relieved.
How precious did that grace appear,
The hour I first believed.

3. Through many dangers, toils, and snares,
I have already come.
'Tis grace that brough me safe thus far,
And grace will lead me home.

4. How sweet the name of Jesus sounds,
In a believer's ear.
It soothes his sorrow, heals his wounds,
And drives away his fear.

5. When we've been there ten thousand years,
Bright shining as the sun,
We've no less days to sing God's praise,
Then when we first begun.

Two Veterans

THE LAST SUNBEAM
Lightly falls from the finished Sabbath,
On the pavement here, and there beyond it is looking
    Down a new-made double grave.

    Lo! the moon ascending,
Up from the east the silvery round moon,
Beautiful over the house-tops, ghastly, phantom moon,
    Immense and silent moon.

    I see a sad procession,
And I hear the sound of coming full-keyed bugles,
All the channels of the city streets they're flooding,
    As with voices and with tears.

    I hear the great drums pounding,
And the small drums steady whirring,
And every blow of the great convulsive drums
    Strikes me through and through.

    For the son is brought with the father,
(In the foremost ranks of the fierce assault they fell,
Two veterans, son and father, dropt together,
    And the double grave awaits them).

    Now nearer blow the bugles,
And the drums strike more convulsive,
And the daylight o'er the pavement quite has faded,
    And the strong dead-march enwraps me.

    In the eastern sky up-buoying,
The sorrowful vast phantom moves illumined,
('Tis some mother's large transparent face
    In heaven brighter growing).

    O strong dead-march you please me!
O moon immense with your silvery face you soothe me!
O my soldiers twain! O my veterans passing to burial!
    What I have I also give you.

    The moon gives you light,
And the bugles and the drums give you music,
And my heart, O my soldiers, my veterans,
    My heart gives you love.

WALT WHITMAN

You're a Grand Old Flag

Words and music by
George M. Cohan

With spirit

You're a grand old flag you're a high fly-ing flag, And for-

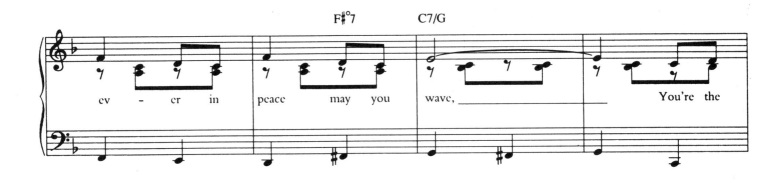

ev-er in peace may you wave, _____ You're the

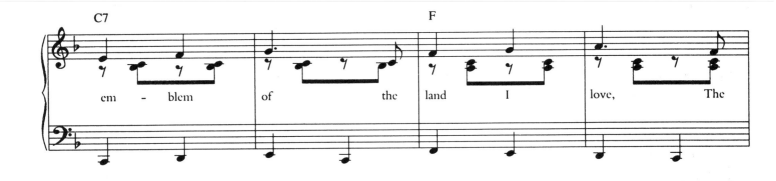

em-blem of the land I love, The

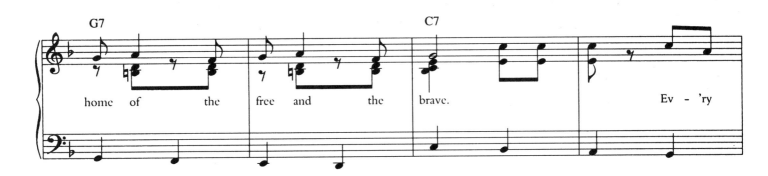

home of the free and the brave. Ev-'ry

The Red, White, and Blue
Columbia, the Gem of the Ocean

Words and music by
Thomas A. Becket and David T. Shaw

Freedom's Banner

WHEN FREEDOM from her mountain height
    Unfurled her standard to the air,
She tore the azure robe of night,
    And set the stars of glory there.

She mingled with its gorgeous dyes
The milky baldric of the skies,
And striped its pure, celestial white,
With streakings of the morning light;
Then from his mansion in the sun
She called her eagle bearer down,
And gave into his mighty hand
The symbol of her chosen land. . . .

Flag of the free heart's hope and home!
    By angel hands to valor given;
Thy stars have lit the welkin dome,
    And all thy hues were born in heaven.
Forever float that standard sheet!
    Where breathes the foe but falls before us,
With Freedom's soil beneath our feet,
    And Freedom's banner streaming o'er us!

FROM *THE AMERICAN FLAG* BY JOSEPH RODMAN DRAKE

Dear Old Daddy Whiskers

Traditional

2. We have a dear old Mommy,
   She likes his whiskers, too.
   She uses them for cleaning
   And stirring up a stew.
   Chorus

3. We have a dear old brother,
   Who has a Ford machine.
   He uses Daddy's whiskers
   To strain the gasoline.
   Chorus

4. We have a dear old sister.
   Her name is Ida Mae.
   She climbs up Daddy's whiskers
   And braids them every day.
   Chorus

5. Around the supper table,
   We make a merry group,
   Until dear Daddy's whiskers
   Get tangled in the soup.
   Chorus

6. Daddy was in battle,
   He wasn't killed, you see:
   His whiskers looked like bushes,
   And fooled the enemy.
   Chorus

7. When Daddy goes in swimming,
   No bathing suit for him.
   He ties his whiskers round his waist,
   And happily jumps in.
   Chorus

For He's a Jolly Good Fellow

Traditional

The Quiet Life

Happy the man, whose wish and care
A few paternal acres bound,
Content to breathe his native air
            In his own ground.

Whose herds with milk, whose fields with bread,
Whose flocks supply him with attire;
Whose trees in summer yield him shade,
            In winter, fire.

Blest, who can unconcern'dly find
Hours, days, and years slide soft away
In health of body, peace of mind,
            Quiet by day,

Sound sleep by night; study and ease
Together mixed; sweet recreation,
And innocence, which most does please
            With meditation.

ALEXANDER POPE

Yankee Doodle

Traditional

Brightly

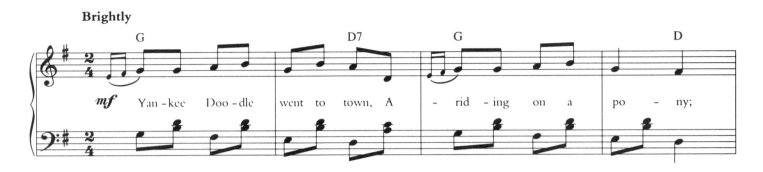

Yan-kee Doo-dle went to town, A-rid-ing on a po-ny;

Stuck a feath-er in his cap, And called it mac-a-ro-ni.

Chorus

Yan-kee Doo-dle keep it up, Yan-kee Doo-dle dan-dy,

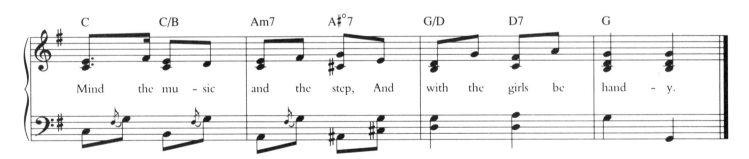

Mind the mu-sic and the step, And with the girls be hand-y.

2. Father and I went down to camp,
   Along with Captain Gooding;
   There we saw the men and boys,
   As thick as hasty pudding.
   Chorus

3. And there we saw a thousand men,
   As rich as Squire David;
   And what they wasted ev'ry day,
   I wish it could be savèd.
   Chorus

4. And there was Captain Washington,
   Upon a slapping stallion,
   A-giving order to his men;
   I guess there was a million.
   Chorus

5. But I can't tell you half I saw,
   They kept up such a smother;
   So I took my hat off, made a bow,
   And scampered home to mother.
   Chorus

THE GLORIOUS FOURTH

The Star-Spangled Banner

Words by Francis Scott Key
Music by John Stafford Smith

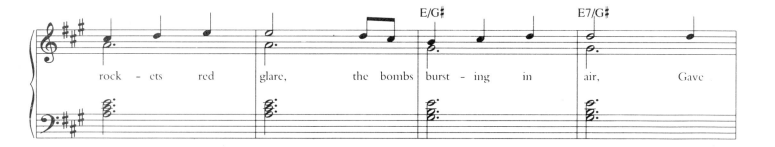

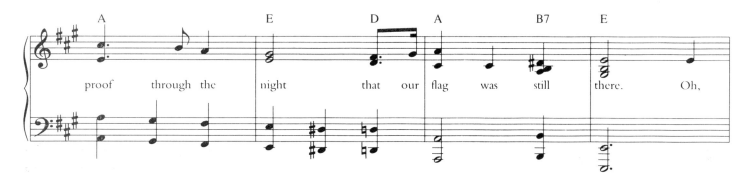

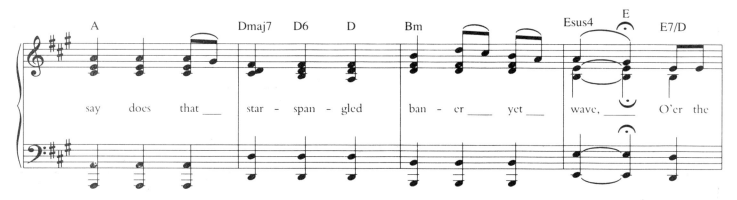

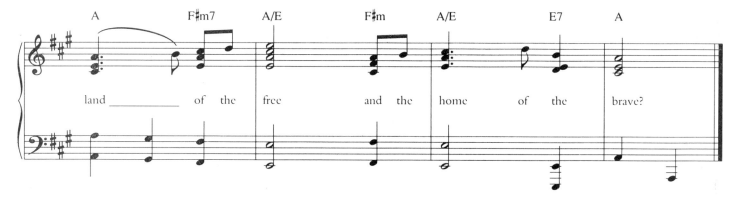

2. On the shore, dimly seen through the mists of the deep,
   Where the foe's haughty host in dread silence reposes,
   What is that which the breeze, o'er the towering steep,
   As it fitfully blows half conceals, half discloses?
   Now it catches the gleam of the morning's first beam,
   In full glory reflected now shines on the stream;
   'Tis the Star-Spangled Banner, oh long may it wave,
   O'er the land of the free and the home of the brave.

3. Oh, thus be it ever when freemen shall stand
   Between their loved homes and the war's desolation.
   Blest with vict'ry and peace, may the heav'n-rescued land
   Praise the Pow'r that hath made and preserved us a nation.
   Then conquer we must, when our cause it is just,
   And this be our motto, "In God is our trust."
   And the Star-Spangled Banner in triumph shall wave,
   O'er the land of the free and the home of the brave.

Concord Hymn

On a Battle Monument, dedicated April 19, 1836

BY THE RUDE BRIDGE that arched the flood,
    Their flag to April's breeze unfurled,
Here once the embattled farmers stood,
    And fired the shot heard round the world.

The foe long since in silence slept;
    Alike the conqueror silent sleeps;
And Time the ruined bridge has swept
    Down the dark stream which seaward creeps.

On the green bank, by this soft stream,
    We set today a votive stone;
That memory may her dead redeem,
    When, like our sires, our sons are gone.

Spirit, that made those heroes dare
    To die, and leave their children free,
Bid Time and Nature gently spare
    The shaft we raise to them and thee.

RALPH WALDO EMERSON

Barbecued Baby Beef Ribs

6 pounds baby beef ribs
Juice of 1 lemon
Salt
Pepper
2 cloves garlic, thinly sliced
1 medium onion, chopped
3 tablespoons butter
1 tablespoon vinegar
2 tablespoons molasses
2 tablespoons prepared mustard
½ cup catsup
2 tablespoons Worcestershire sauce
1 tablespoon Liquid Smoke
Few drops of Tabasco sauce

1. Preheat the oven to 350°F.

2. Place the racks of ribs in a baking pan and squeeze a lemon over them. Season with salt and pepper.

3. In a saucepan, sauté the garlic and onion in the butter. Add the remaining ingredients, and stir until the mixture begins to boil.

4. Spread the sauce over the ribs and bake for at least 1½ hours.

To prepare on outdoor barbecue grill:
Squeeze a lemon over the rib racks, then season them with salt and pepper. Place the racks of ribs on a hot grill. Prepare barbecue sauce as above, but omit Liquid Smoke. Grill ribs until done on one side, then turn each rack, and brush with barbecue sauce. When done on that side, brush the tops with barbecue sauce, and turn once again. Grill five more minutes, then serve.

Serves 6.

Spicy Stuffed Eggs

8 extra-large eggs
3 teaspoons prepared mustard
½ teaspoon powdered horseradish
2 tablespoons mayonnaise
4 ripe black olives, minced
½ teaspoon salt
Paprika

1. Place the eggs in a saucepan and cover with cold water. Bring slowly to a boil. Reduce the heat, cover, and simmer for 20 minutes. Drain. Crack the eggs by shaking them against the sides of the pan. Place the eggs in cold water. Refrigerate. The shells will slip right off when ready to use.

2. Cut the eggs in half and gently remove yolks. Mash the yolks with the mustard, horseradish, mayonnaise, olives, and salt. Scoop yolk mixture back into the white halves, sprinkle with paprika, and chill until served.

Serves 6 to 8.

Santa Lucia

Italian Air

In my light gon-do-la, at close of day, When twi-light's fall - ing
Na-ples so beau-ti-ful ly-ing be-fore me, All thy sons dut-i-ful
Sul ma-re luc-ci-ca l'a-stro d'ar-gen-to Gla-ci-da e l'on-da

o-ver the bright bay, Sil-ver stars shin-ing on the blue sea,
love and a-dore thee. Light-ly the ev-'ning wind's blow-ing to sea,
pros-pero e il ven-to Sul ma-re luc-ci-ca l'a-stro d'ar-gen-to

In this sweet lone-ly hour, I think of thee. May the good an - gels
Bright-ly I'm has-ten - ing, row-ing to thee. May the good an - gels
Gla - ci - da e l'on - da pros-pero e il ven - to Ven - ite all' a - gi - le

guard and pro - tect us, San - ta Lu - ci - a, aid and di - rect us! Bless our fi -
guard and pro - tect us, San - ta Lu - ci - a, aid and di - rect us! Rul - er of
Bar - chet - ta mi - a San - ta Lu - ci - a, San - ta Lu - ci - a Ven - ite all'

del - i - ty, bring us pros - per - i - ty, San - ta Lu - ci - a, San - ta Lu - ci - a!
harmony, send me good company, San - ta Lu - ci - a, San - ta Lu - ci - a!
a - gi - le Bar - chet - te mi - a San - ta Lu - ci - a, San - ta Lu - ci - a!

Funiculi, Funicula

Words and music by Luigi Denza

Antipasto Salad

1 small head cauliflower, cut into florets
2 ounces black olives, sliced
2 ounces green olives stuffed with pimientos (whole)
6 cherry tomatoes
2 ounces anchovy filets, drained
1 pound canned garbanzo beans
2 hard-boiled eggs, sliced
6 scallions, chopped
Sprigs of dill (for garnish)

Dressing:
½ cup olive oil
¼ cup vinegar
1 teaspoon garlic salt (or table salt)
1 teaspoon freshly ground pepper

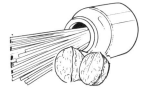

1. Place the cauliflower in a saucepan and pour boiling water over it. Allow it to stand a few minutes to soften the florets, then drain.

2. Shake or mix dressing ingredients together.

3. Combine the cauliflower with the olives, tomatoes, anchovies, garbanzo beans, eggs, and onions. Add dressing and toss very gently. Garnish with springs of dill.

Serves 6 to 8.

Spinach Fettucine With Walnuts

4 tablespoons butter
½ cup chopped walnuts
½ cup seasoned dry bread crumbs
1 clove garlic, thinly sliced
2 tablespoons chopped parsley
One 8-ounce package medium-wide noodles

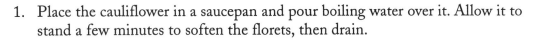

1. Melt the butter in a skillet. Add the walnuts, bread crumbs, and garlic and cook over low heat until the garlic is golden brown. Stir in the parsley.

2. Cook noodles in boiling salted water. Drain and place in a serving bowl.

3. Pour the nut mixture over the noodles. Toss and serve immediately.

Serves 6.

Jack-o-Lantern

Words by Amy Appleby and Peter Pickow
Music Traditional

Haunted

From out the wood I watched them shine—
The windows of the haunted house,
Now ruddy as enchanted wine,
Now dim as flittermouse.

There went a thin voice piping airs
Along the grey and crooked walks—
A garden of thistledown and tares,
Bright leaves, and giant stalks.

The twilight rain shone at its gates,
Where long-leaved grass in shadow grew;
And black in silence to her mates
A voiceless raven flew.

Lichen and moss the lone stones greened,
Green paths led lightly to its door,
Keen from her lair the spider leaned,
And dusk to darkness wore.

Amidst the sedge a whisper ran,
The West shut down a heavy eye,
And like last tapers, few and wan,
The watch-stars kindled in the sky.

WALTER DE LA MARE

Funeral March of a Marionette

Charles Gounod

Mysteriously

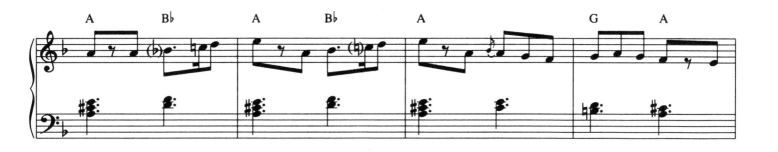

The Kitten and Falling Leaves

SEE THE KITTEN on the wall,
Sporting with the leaves that fall,
Withered leaves—one—two—and three—
From the lofty elder tree!
Through the calm and frosty air
Of this morning bright and fair,
Eddying round and round they sink
Softly, slowly: one might think
From the motions that are made,
Every little leaf conveyed
Sylph or fairy hither tending,
To this lower world descending,
Each invisible and mute,
In his wavering parachute.
But the kitten, how she starts,
Crouches, stretches, paws and darts!
First at one and then its fellow,
Just as light and just as yellow;
There are many now—now one—
Now they stop and there are none:
What intenseness of desire
In her upward eye of fire!
With a tiger-leap, half-way,
Now she meets the coming prey;
Lets it go as fast and then
Has it in her power again.
Now she works with three or four,
Like an Indian conjuror;
Quick as he in feats of art
Far beyond in joy of heart.

WILLIAM WORDSWORTH

Popcorn Balls

12 cups popped corn
1 cup peanuts
1 cup light corn syrup
½ cup brown sugar
1 tablespoon white vinegar
¼ cup butter
Colored cellophane

1. Grease a large mixing bowl with butter. Toss popcorn and peanuts together.

2. In a saucepan, heat corn syrup, brown sugar, and vinegar, stirring constantly, until the mixture begins to boil. Allow to boil on medium heat until a drop of the mixture hardens to a ball when tested in cold water.

3. Remove from heat and stir in the butter.

4. Pour the syrup over the popcorn and peanuts and toss.

5. Butter hands and shape mixture into 3″ balls. Put each ball on waxed paper to dry, then wrap individually in colored cellophane.

Makes 20 balls.

Caramel Apples

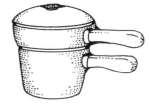

8 medium Delicious apples
Two 14-ounce packages of soft caramel candies
1 teaspoon salt
1/4 cup butter
Wooden skewers

1. In a double boiler, heat the caramel, salt, and butter, stirring constantly, until well-blended.

2. Remove stems from apples and stick one wooden skewer in the center of each apple at the stem end. While the sauce is still on the stove, twirl each apple in the caramel mixture. Use a spoon to coat each apple completely.

3. Place each apple on waxed paper once it has been coated, with skewers pointing up.

4. Chill until ready to serve.

Makes 8 caramel apples.

The Headless Horseman

THERE WAS A CONTAGION in the very air that blew from that haunted region; it breathed forth an atmosphere of dreams and fancies infecting all the land. Several of the Sleepy Hollow people were present at Van Tassel's, and, as usual, were doling out their wild and wonderful legends. Many dismal tales were told about funeral trains, and mourning cries and wailings heard and seen about the great tree where the unfortunate Major André was taken, and which stood in the neighborhood. Some mention was made also of the woman in white, that haunted the dark glen at Raven Rock, and was often heard to shriek on winter nights before a storm, having perished there in the snow. The chief part of the stories, however, turned upon the favorite spectre of Sleepy Hollow, the headless horseman, who had been heard several times of late, patrolling the country; and, it was said, tethered his horse nightly among the graves in the churchyard.

The sequestered situation of this church seems always to have made it a favorite haunt of troubled spirits. It stands on a knoll, surrounded by locust-trees and lofty elms, from among which its decent whitewashed walls shine modestly forth, like Christian purity beaming through the shades of retirement. A gentle slope descends from it to a silver sheet of water, bordered by high trees, between which, peeps may be caught at the blue hills of the Hudson. To look upon its grass-grown yard, where the sunbeams seem to sleep so quietly, one would think that there at least the dead might rest in peace. On one side of the church extends a wide woody dell, along which raves a large brook among broken rocks and trunks of fallen trees. Over a deep, black part of the stream, not far from the church, was formerly thrown a wooden bridge; the road that led to it, and the bridge itself, were thickly shaded by overhanging trees, which cast a gloom about it, even in the daytime; but occasioned a fearful darkness at night. This was one of the favorite haunts of the headless horseman; and the place where he was most frequently encountered. The tale was told of old Brouwer, a most heretical disbeliever in ghosts, how he met the horseman returning from his foray into Sleepy Hollow, and was obliged to get up behind him; how they galloped over bush and brake, over hill and swamp, until they reached the bridge; when the horseman suddenly turned into a skeleton, threw old Brouwer into the brook, and sprang away over the tree-tops with a clap of thunder.

This story was immediately matched by a thrice marvellous adventure of Brom Bones, who made light of the galloping Hessian as an arrant jockey. He affirmed that, on returning one night from the neighboring village of Sing-Sing; he had been overtaken by this midnight trooper; that he had offered to race with him for a bowl of punch, and should have won it too, for Daredevil beat the goblin horse all hollow, but, just as they came to the church bridge, the Hessian bolted, and vanished in a flash of fire.

All these tales, told in that drowsy undertone with which men talk in the dark, the countenances of the listeners only now and then receiving a casual gleam from the glare of a pipe, sank deep in the mind of Ichabod. He repaid them in kind with large extracts from his invaluable author, Cotton Mather, and added many marvellous events that had taken place in his native State of Connecticut, and fearful sights which he had seen in his nightly walks about Sleepy Hollow.

The revel now gradually broke up. The old farmers gathered together their families in their wagons, and were heard for some times rattling along the hollow roads and over the distant hills. Some of the damsels mounted on pillions behind their favorite swains, and their light-hearted laughter, mingling with the clatter of hoofs, echoed along the silent woodlands, sounding fainter and fainter until they gradually died away—and the scene of noise and frolic was all silent. . . .

It was the very witching time of night that Ichabod Crane, heavy-hearted and crest-fallen, pursued his travel homewards, along the sides of the lofty hills which rise above Tarrytown, and which he had traversed so cheerily in the afternoon. The hour was as dismal as himself. Far below him, the Tappan Zee spread its dusky and indistinct waste of waters, with here and there the tall mast of a sloop riding quietly at anchor under the land. In the dead hush of midnight, he could even hear the barking of the watch-dog from the opposite shore of the Hudson; but it was so vague and faint as only to give an idea of his distance from this faithful companion of man. Now and then, too, the long-drawn crowing of a cock, accidentally awakened, would sound far, far off, from some farmhouse away among the hills—but it was like a dreaming sound in his ear. No signs of life occurred near him, but occasionally the melancholy chirp of a cricket, or perhaps the guttural twang of a bullfrog from a neighboring marsh, as if sleeping uncomfortably and turning suddenly in his bed.

All the stories of ghosts and goblins that he had heard in the afternoon, now came crowding upon his recollection. The night grew darker and darker; the stars seemed to sink deeper in the sky, and driving clouds occasionally hid them from his sight. He had never felt so lonely and dismal. He was, moreover, approaching the very place where many of the scenes of the ghost stories had been laid. In the centre of the road stood an enormous tulip-tree, which towered like a giant above all the other trees of the neighborhood, and formed a kind of landmark. Its limbs were gnarled, and fantastic, large enough to form trunks for ordinary trees, twisting down almost to the earth, and rising again into the air. It was connected with the tragical story of the unfortunate André, who had been taken prisoner hard by; and was universally known by the name of Major André's tree. The common people regarded it with a mixture of respect and superstition, partly out of sympathy for the fate of its ill-starred namesake, and partly from the tales of strange sights and doleful lamentations told concerning it.

As Ichabod approached this fearful tree, he began to whistle: he thought his whistle was answered—it was but a blast sweeping sharply through the dry branches. As he approached a little nearer, he thought he saw something white hanging in the midst of the tree—he paused and ceased whistling; but on looking more narrowly, perceived that it was a place where the tree had been scathed by lightning, and the white wood laid bare. Suddenly he heard a groan—his teeth chattered and his knees smote against the saddle: it was but the rubbing of one huge bough upon another, as they were swayed about by the breeze. He passed the tree in safety, but new perils lay before him.

About two hundred yards from the tree a small brook crossed the road, and ran into a marshy and thickly-wooded glen, known by the name of Wiley's swamp. A few rough logs, laid side by side, served for a bridge over this stream. On that side of the road where the brook entered the wood, a group of oaks and chestnuts, matted thick with wild grape-vines, threw a cavernous gloom over it. To pass this bridge was the severest trial. It was at this identical spot that the unfortunate André was captured, and under the covert of those chestnuts and vines were the sturdy yeomen concealed who surprised him. This has ever since been considered a haunted stream, and fearful are the feelings of the schoolboy who has to pass it alone after dark.

As he approached the stream his heart began to thump; he summoned up, however, all his resolution, gave his horse half a score of kicks in the ribs, and attempted to dash briskly across the bridge; but instead of starting forward, the perverse old animal made a lateral movement, and ran broadside against the fence. Ichabod, whose fears increased with the delay jerked the reins on the other side, and kicked lustily with the contrary fact: it was all in vain; his steed started, it is true, but it was only to plunge to the opposite side of the road into a thicket of brambles and alder bushes. The schoolmaster now bestowed both whip and heel upon the starveling ribs of old Gunpowder, who dashed forward, snuffling and snorting, but came to a stand just by the bridge, with a suddenness that had nearly sent his rider sprawling over his head. Just at this moment a plashy tramp by the side of the bridge caught the sensitive ear of Ichabod. In the dark shadow of the grove, on the margin of the brook, he beheld something huge, misshapen, black and towering. It stirred not, but seemed gathered up in the gloom, like some gigantic monster ready to spring upon the traveller.

The hair of the affrighted pedagogue rose upon his head with terror. What was to be done? To turn and fly was now too late; and besides, what chance was there of escaping ghost or goblin, if such it was, which could ride upon the wings of the wind? Summoning up, therefore, a show of courage, he demanded in stammering accents—"Who are you?" He received no reply. He repeated his demand in a still more agitated voice. Still there was no answer. Once more he cudgelled the sides of the inflexible Gunpowder, and, shutting his eyes, broke forth with involuntary fervor into a psalm tune. Just then the shadowy object of alarm put itself in motion, and, with a scramble and a bound, stood at once in the middle of the road. Though the night was dark and dismal, yet the form of the unknown might now in some degree be ascertained. He appeared to be a horseman of large dimensions, and mounted on a black horse of powerful frame. He made no offer of molestation or sociability, but kept aloof on one side of the road, jogging along on the blind side of old Gunpowder, who had now got over his fright and waywardness.

Ichabod, who had no relish for this strange midnight companion, and bethought himself of the adventure of Brom Bones and the Galloping Hessian, now quickened his steed, in hopes of leaving him behind. The stranger, however, quickened his horse to an equal pace. Ichabod pulled up, and fell into a walk, thinking to lag behind—the other did the same. His heart began to sink within him; he endeavored to resume his psalm tune, but his parched tongue clove to the roof of his mouth, and he could not utter a stave. There was something in the moody and dogged silence of this pertinacious companion, that was mysterious and appalling. It was soon fearfully accounted for. On mounting a rising ground, which brought the figure of his fellow-traveller in relief against the sky, gigantic in height, and muffled in a cloak, Ichabod was horror-struck, on perceiving that he was headless!—but his horror was still more increased, on observing that the head, which should have rested on his shoulders, was carried before him on the pommel of the saddle: his terror rose to desperation; he rained a shower of kicks and blows upon Gunpowder, hoping, by a sudden movement, to give his companion the slip—but the spectre started full jump with him. Away then they dashed through thick and thin; stones flying, and sparks flashing at every bound. Ichabod's flimsy garments fluttered in the air, as he stretched his long, lank body away over his horse's head, in the eagerness of his flight.

They had now reached the road which turns off to Sleepy Hollow; but Gunpowder, who seemed possessed with a demon, instead of keeping up it, made an opposite turn, and plunged headlong down hill to the left. This road leads through a sandy hollow, shaded by trees for about a quarter of a mile, where it crosses the bridge famous in goblin story, and just beyond swells the green knoll on which stands the whitewashed church. As yet the panic of the steed had given his unskilful rider an apparent advantage in the chase; but just as he had got half way through the hollow, the girths of the saddle gave way, and he felt it slipping from under him. He seized it by the pommel, and endeavored to hold it firm, but in vain; and had just time to save himself by clasping old Gunpowder round the neck, when the saddle fell to the earth, and he heard it trampled under foot by his pursuer. For a moment the terror of Hans Van Ripper's wrath passed across his mind—for it was his Sunday saddle; but this was no time for petty fears; the goblin was hard on his haunches; and (unskilful rider that he was!) he had much ado to maintain his seat; sometimes slipping on one side, sometimes on another, and sometimes jolted on the high ridge of his horse's backbone, with a violence that he verily feared would cleave him asunder.

An opening in the trees now cheered him with the hopes that the church bridge was at hand. The wavering reflection of a silver star in the bosom of the brook told him that he was not mistaken. He saw the walls of the church dimly glaring under the trees beyond. He recollected the place where Brom Bones's ghostly competitor had disappeared. "If I can but reach that bridge," thought Ichabod, "I am safe." Just then he heard the black steed panting and blowing close behind him; he even fancied that he felt his hot breath. Another convulsive kick in the ribs, and old Gunpowder sprang upon the bridge; he thundered over the resounding planks; he gained the opposite side; and now Ichabod cast a look behind to see if his pursuer should vanish, according to rule, in a flash of fire and brimstone. Just then he saw the goblin rising in his stirrups, and in the very act of hurling his head at him. Ichabod endeavored to dodge this horrible missile, but too late. It encountered his cranium with a tremendous crash—he was tumbled headlong into the dust, and Gunpowder, the black steed, and the goblin rider passed by like a whirlwind.

The next morning the old horse was found without his saddle, and with the bridle under his feet, soberly cropping the grass at his master's gate. Ichabod did not make his appearance at breakfast—dinner-hour came, but no Ichabod. The boys assembled at the school-house, and strolled idly about the banks of the brook; but no school-master. Hans Van Ripper now began to feel some uneasiness about the fate of poor Ichabod, and his saddle. An inquiry was set on foot, and after diligent investigation they came upon his traces. In one part of the road leading to the church was found the saddle trampled in the dirt; the tracks of horses' hoofs deeply dented in the road, and evidently at furious speed, were traced to the bridge, beyond which, on the bank of a broad part of the brook, where the water ran deep and black, was found the hat of the unfortunate Ichabod, and close beside it a shattered pumpkin.

FROM *THE LEGEND OF SLEEPY HOLLOW* BY WASHINGTON IRVING

Anchors Aweigh

Words by Alred Hart Miles and R. Lovell
Music by Charles A. Zimmerman

Brightly

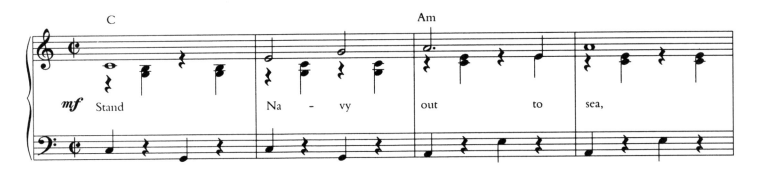

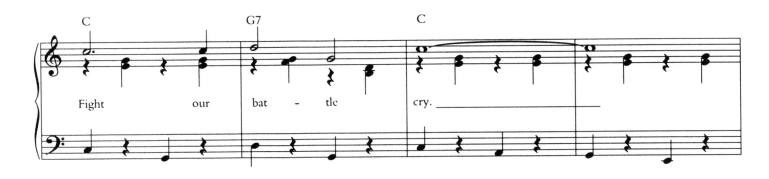

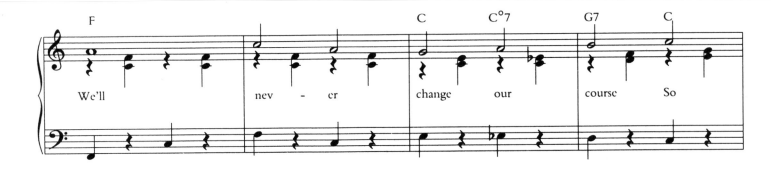

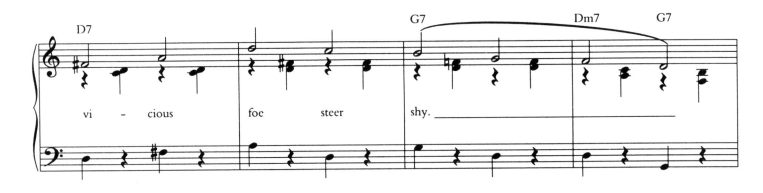

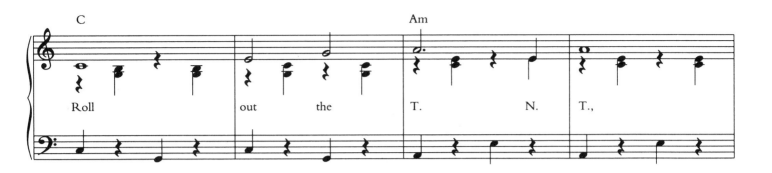

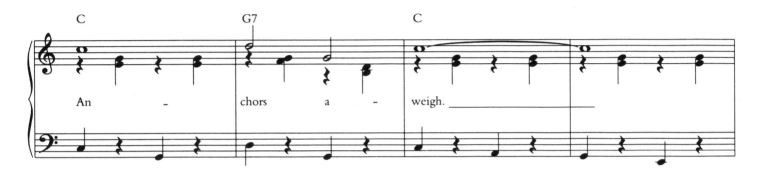

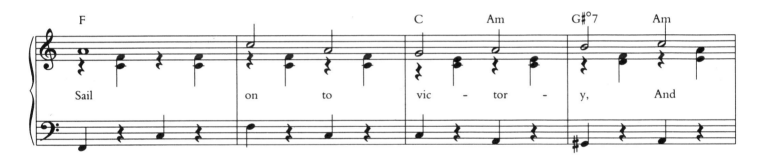

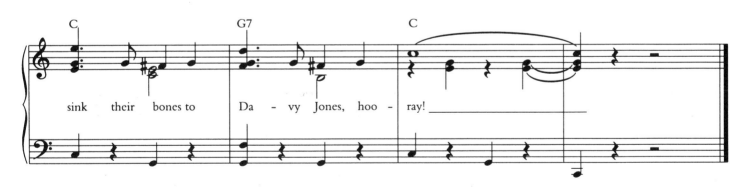

College Version

1. Anchors aweigh, my boys,
   Anchors aweigh.
   Farewell to college joys,
   We sail at break of day.
   Through our last night on shore,
   Drink to the foam;
   Until we meet once more,
   Here's wishing you a happy voyage home.

2. Stand, Navy, down the field
   Sail to the sky.
   We'll never change our course,
   So, Army, you steer shy.
   Roll up the score, Navy,
   Anchors aweigh.
   Sail, Navy, down the field,
   And sink the Army, sink the Army Grey.

The Caissons Go Rolling Along

Words and music by Edmund L. Gruber

With movement

The Marines' Hymn

Words Anonymous
Music from Jacques Offenbach's *Geneviève de Brabant*

Courageously

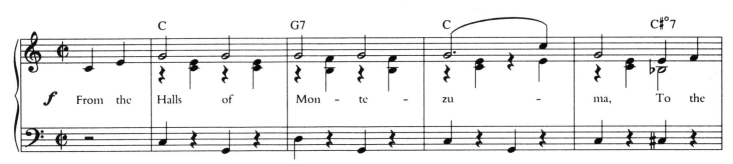

f From the Halls of Mon - te - zu - ma, To the

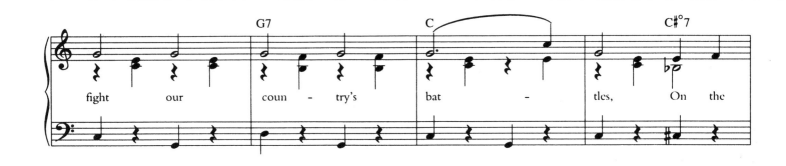

shores of Tri - po - li, We

fight our coun - try's bat - tles, On the

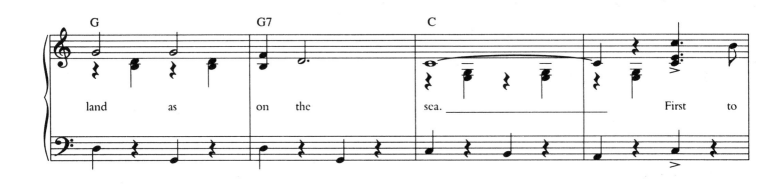

land as on the sea. First to

fight for right and free - dom, And to

keep our hon - or clean, _____ We are

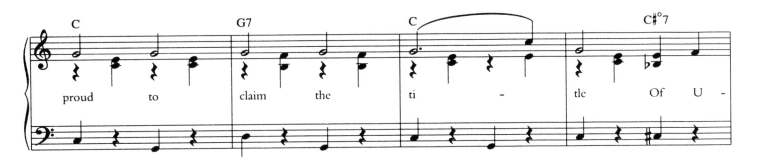

proud to claim the ti - tle Of U -

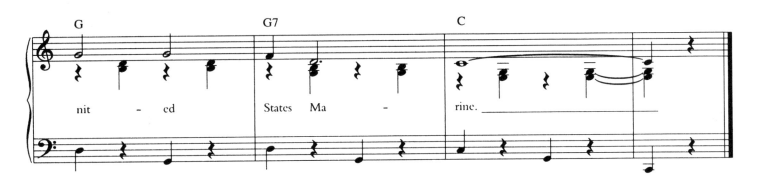

nit - ed States Ma - rine. _____

2. Our flag's unfurled to every breeze,
From dawn to setting sun.
We have fought in every clime and place,
Where we could take a gun.
In the snow of far-off Northern lands,
And in sunny tropic scenes,
You will find us always on the job,
The United States Marines.

3. Here's health to you and to our Corps,
Which we are proud to serve.
In many a strife we've fought for life,
And never lost our nerve.
If the Army and the Navy,
Ever look on Heaven's scenes,
They will find the streets are guarded,
By United States Marines.

Over the River and Through the Wood

Traditional

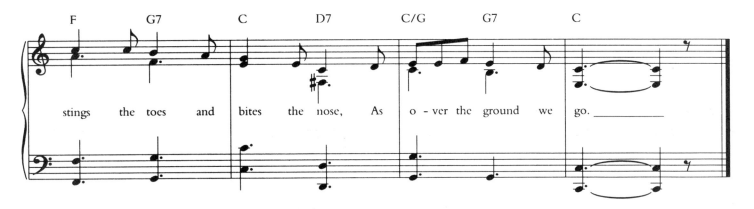

stings   the toes   and   bites   the nose,   As   o - ver the ground   we   go. _____

2. Over the river and through the wood,
   To have a full day of play.
   Oh, hear the bells ringing "ting-a-ling ling,"
   For it's Thanksgiving Day.
   Over the river and through the wood,
   Trot fast, my dapple gray.
   Spring o'er the ground just like a hound.
   Hurrah for Thanksgiving Day!

3. Over the river and through the wood,
   And straight through the barnyard gate.
   It seems that we go so dreadfully slow,
   It is so hard to wait.
   Over the river and through the wood,
   Now grandma's cap I spy.
   Hurrah for fun, the pudding's done,
   Hurrah for the pumpkin pie!

Pumpkin Pie

1 can pumpkin (2 cups)
1 teaspoon cinnamon
½ teaspoon nutmeg
½ teaspoon ground cloves
½ teaspoon ginger
¼ teaspoon salt
2 eggs, beaten
¾ cup light brown sugar (packed)
1⅔ cup light cream

Pastry:
½ teaspoon salt
1 cup all-purpose flour
⅓ cup shortening
1 tablespoon butter
3 tablespoons cold water (or less)

1. Preheat the oven to 425°F.

2. To prepare the pastry: Mix the salt with the flour and cut in the shortening until the mixture is the consistency of coarse cornmeal. Gradually add cold water until a dough forms. Roll the dough into a ball and chill for 30 minutes.

3. In a large mixing bowl blend pumpkin, cinnamon, nutmeg, cloves, ginger, and salt. Gradually add beaten eggs, sugar, and cream. Beat until well-blended.

4. Roll out the ball of dough into a circle and place in lightly greased 9″ pie pan. Crimp around the edges with a fork. Pour the pumpkin filling into this crust. Place the pie pan on a cookie sheet to avoid oven spills. Bake for 15 minutes.

5. Reduce the oven temperature to 350°F. Bake 45 minutes longer, or until a knife inserted in the filling comes out clean. Allow to cool. (Top with whipped cream before serving, if desired.)

Serves 6 to 8.

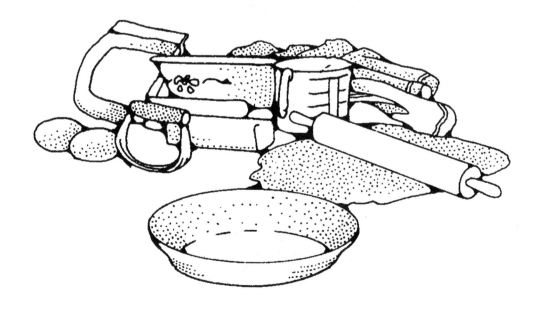

Prayer of Thanksgiving

Traditional

With reverence

We gath - er to - geth - er, To ask the Lord's bless - ing; He chas - tens and has - tens, His will to make known; The wick - ed op - pres - sing, Cease them _____ from dis - tres - sing, Sing prais - es to His name, He for - gets not his own.

2. Beside us to guide us,
Our God with us joining,
Ordaining, maintaining
His kingdom divine;
So from the beginning,
The fight we were winning,
Thou, Lord, wast at our side,
Let the glory be Thine.

3. We all do extol Thee,
Thou leader in battle,
And pray that Thou still
Our defender will be.
Let Thy congregation
Escape tribulation.
Thy name be ever praised,
And Thy people be free.

Shine On Harvest Moon

Words by Jack Norworth
Music by Nora Bayes and Jack Norworth

Five Fat Turkeys

Traditional

Oh, five **fat tur**-keys are we_____ We
slept all night in a **tree.** When the cook came a-round, We
could-n't be found, And that's why we're here, You see._____

A Hungry Cat's Thanksgiving

IT WAS A hungry pussy cat,
Upon Thanksgiving morn,
And she watched a thankful little mouse,
That ate an ear of corn.

"If I ate that thankful little mouse,
How thankful he should be,
When he has made a meal himself,
To make a meal for me!

"Then with his thanks for having fed,
And his thanks for feeding me,
With all *his* thankfulness inside,
How thankful I shall be!"

Thus mused the hungry pussy cat,
Upon Thanksgiving Day;
But the little mouse had overheard,
And declined (with thanks) to stay.

OLIVER HERFORD

Roast Turkey With Sage Dressing

One 12- to 16-pound turkey
Vegetable oil
2 onions, peeled and sliced
4 stalks celery, sliced
1 tablespoon flour

Gravy:
½ cup turkey juices
1 tablespoon flour
2 cups cold water (or milk)
Salt
Pepper

Sage Dressing:
½ cup melted butter
½ cup minced onion
4 cups herb-seasoned bread cubes (one 7-ounce package)
1 cup chicken stock
1 egg, beaten
2 tablespoons sage
Chopped turkey giblets (optional)
Salt
Pepper

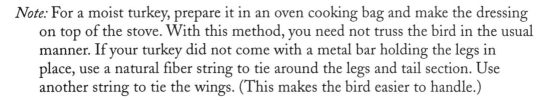

Note: For a moist turkey, prepare it in an oven cooking bag and make the dressing on top of the stove. With this method, you need not truss the bird in the usual manner. If your turkey did not come with a metal bar holding the legs in place, use a natural fiber string to tie around the legs and tail section. Use another string to tie the wings. (This makes the bird easier to handle.)

1. Preheat the oven 350°F. Wash the turkey and pat dry. Rub with oil and stuff with slices of onion and celery. Place 1 tablespoon of flour in a large cooking bag. Add the turkey and close the bag with the nylon tie that comes with it, or with a piece of natural-fiber string. Cut 6 slits in the bag to allow steam to escape. Place the turkey and bag in a roasting pan and insert a meat thermometer into the inside of one thigh (being careful not to let it touch a bone). When the thermometer registers 180°F, the turkey is done. (It will take about 2½ hours for a 12- to 16-pound turkey.) Remove the turkey from the bag and place on a platter. Empty the bag into a large skillet and skim off the juices into a measuring cup. You may wish to serve the hot juice in a sauceboat, after removing most of the fat from the surface, or make gravy.

2. To prepare the gravy: Pour ½ cup of the turkey juices into a frying pan. Add 1 tablespoon of flour and stir until blended and browned. Add a cup of cold water and cook and stir until smooth. Add another cup of cold water and cook and stir. Season with salt and pepper. (You may use cold milk instead of water if you prefer.)

3. Giblets may be used in the gravy or dressing. Simmer the giblets in water until tender. Chop and use as you prefer.

4. To prepare the sage dressing: In a skillet, heat the butter and add the onion and bread cubes. Sauté until the onion is translucent. Add the turkey juices, egg, and sage and mix well. If you wish, add the chopped giblets. Season with salt and pepper. Mix and keep warm over low heat until ready to serve.

Serves 6 to 8.

The Golden Corn

Heap high the farmer's wintry hoard!
  Heap high the golden corn!
No richer gift has Autumn poured
  From out her lavish horn!

Let other lands, exulting, glean
  The apple from the pine,
The orange from its glossy green,
  The cluster from the vine;

We better love the hardy gift
  Our rugged vales bestow,
To cheer us when the storm shall drift
  Our harvest-fields with snow.

Through vales of grass and meads of flowers,
  Our ploughs their furrows made,
While on the hills the sun and showers
  Of changeful April played.

We dropped the seed o'er hill and plain,
  Beneath the sun of May,
And frightened from our sprouting grain
  The robber crows away.

All through the long bright days of June
  Its leaves grew green and fair,
And waved in hot midsummer's noon
  Its soft and yellow hair.

And now with autumn's moonlit eves,
  Its harvest-time has come,
We pluck away the frosted leaves,
  And bear the treasure home.

There richer than the fabled gift
  Apollo showered of old,
Fair hands the broken grain shall sift,
  And knead its meal of gold.

JOHN GREENLEAF WHITTIER

Pilgrims' Cornbread

1 egg
1½ cups milk
1½ tablespoons melted butter
2 cups all-purpose flour
1 cup yellow cornmeal
3 teaspoons baking powder
1 teaspoon salt
2 tablespoons sugar

1. Preheat the oven to 425°F.

2. In a small bowl, beat the egg with a fork. Add the milk and melted butter, mixing well.

3. In a large bowl, place the flour, cornmeal, baking powder, salt and sugar and stir thoroughly with a wooden spoon. (For this batter, the best consistency is achieved with hand mixing.)

4. Gradually pour the milk mixture into the flour mixture, being sure the milk is absorbed by the flour. The dough will be quite sticky. Put into a greased and floured 9″ square pan and bake 20 minutes or until the cornbread begins to separate from the sides of the pan.

Serves 6 to 8.

Hanukkah Song

Traditional

With spirit

Oh, Ha-nuk-kah, oh, Ha-nuk-kah, come light the me-no-rah, Let's have a par-ty, we'll all dance the *ho-ra.* Gath-er 'round the ta-ble, we'll give you a treat, *S'vi-vo-nim* to play with, *le-vi-vot* to eat. And while we are play-ing, The can-dles are burn-ing ___ low;

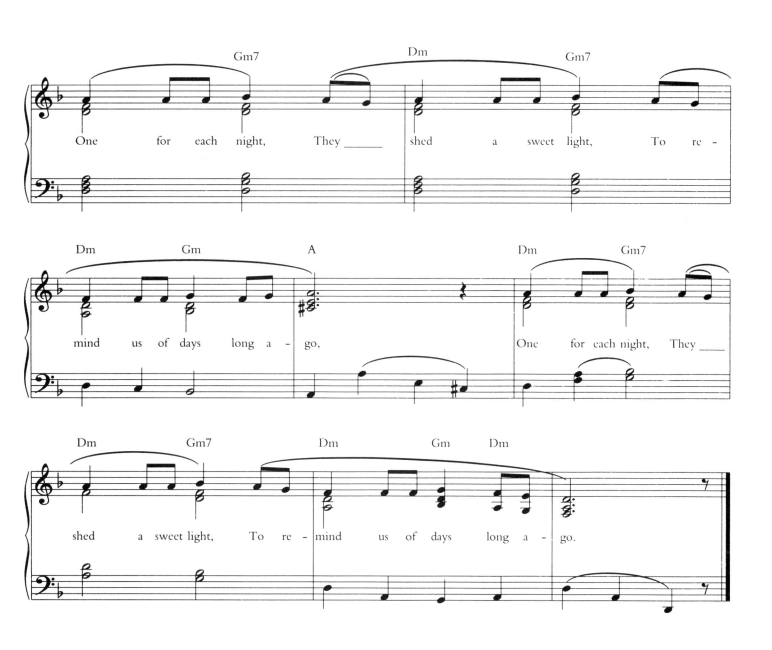

One for each night, They ____ shed a sweet light, To re-
mind us of days long a - go,
One for each night, They ____
shed a sweet light, To re - mind us of days long a - go.

Havah Nagilah

Traditional

Vigorous hora

Lyrics (as set under the music):

Ha - vah nagilah, ha - ah nagilah,
Ha - vah nagilah, vay - nis - m'chayh.
Ha - vah nagilah, hav - ah nagilah,
Hav - ah nagilah, vay - nis - m'chayh.

Somewhat faster

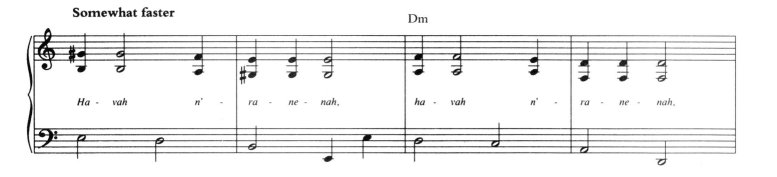

Ha - vah n' - ra - ne - nah, ha - vah n' - ra - ne - nah,

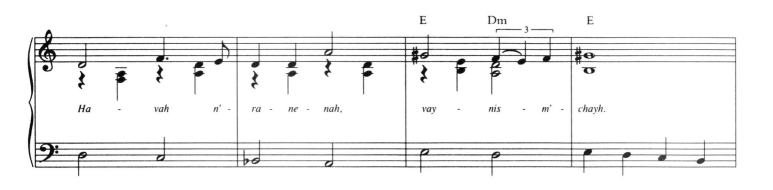

Ha - vah n' - ra - ne - nah, vay - nis - m' - chayh.

Ha - vah n' - ra - ne - nah, ha - vah n' - ra - ne - nah,

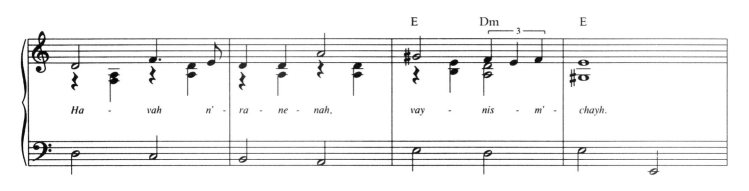

Ha - vah n' - ra - ne - nah, vay - nis - m' - chayh.

U —   ru,   u — ru   a — chim,

octaves optional to end

u-ru a-chim, b'-lev sa—me—ach. U-ru a—chim, b'-lev sa—me—ach.

U-ru a—chim, b'-lev sa—me—ach. U-ru a—chim, b'-lev sa—me—ach.

U-ru a—chim,   b'lev sa—me — ach.

Latkes
Potato Fritters

2 pounds potatoes
1 medium onion
¼ cup chives (or scallions), chopped
1 egg
2 tablespoons matzo meal
½ teaspoon salt
¼ cup margarine (or vegetable oil)
1 pint sour cream (for topping)

1. Peel potatoes (or just remove the eyes) and grate with a food processor or grater, then drain thoroughly. Finely chop the onion.

3. In a large mixing bowl, beat the egg until creamy as you gradually add the matzo meal and salt. Add potatoes, onion, and chives and mix well. Form the potato mixture into 20 small balls, then shape into patties.

4. In a large frying pan, melt margarine over a low heat. Fry one latke at a time, pressing with a spatula to thin each patty into a pancake. When the pancake is golden brown, turn and brown it on the other side.

5. Drain on paper towels and serve with a dollop of sour cream. (Latkes are also traditionally served with applesauce at Hanukkah. You can use store-bought applesauce, or try the delicious homemade recipe below.)

Serves 8 to 10.

Homemade Applesauce

8 medium cooking apples (tart)
1 cup brown sugar
1 cup water
½ teaspoon cinnamon
Juice of 1 lemon

1. Wash, pare, quarter, and core the apples.

2. In a large saucepan, boil the sugar and water for 7 minutes, until a syrup forms.

3. Reduce the heat, add the apples and cook for 10 minutes, stirring occasionally, until tender.

4. Stir in cinnamon and lemon juice, and return to a boil.

5. Purée the mixture in batches in a blender or food processor until smooth. Push through a sieve into a large mixing bowl. Chill and serve with latkes.

Makes 8 cups.

Index of Songs

Index of Readings & Recipes

Readings

Recipes